THE
FORGOTTEN
SOLDIER

THE
FORGOTTEN
SOLDIER

HE WASN'T A SOLDIER, HE WAS JUST A BOY

CHARLIE CONNELLY

HARPER
element

HarperElement
An imprint of HarperCollins*Publishers*
77–85 Fulham Palace Road,
Hammersmith, London W6 8JB

www.harpercollins.co.uk

First published by HarperElement 2014

3

A catalogue record of this book is
available from the British Library

PB ISBN: 978-0-00-758462-8
EB ISBN: 978-0-00-758463-5

Printed and bound in Great Britain by
Clays Ltd, St Ives plc

MIX
Paper from
responsible sources
FSC C007454

Find out more about HarperCollins and the environment at
www.harpercollins.co.uk/green

For Edward Charles Manco

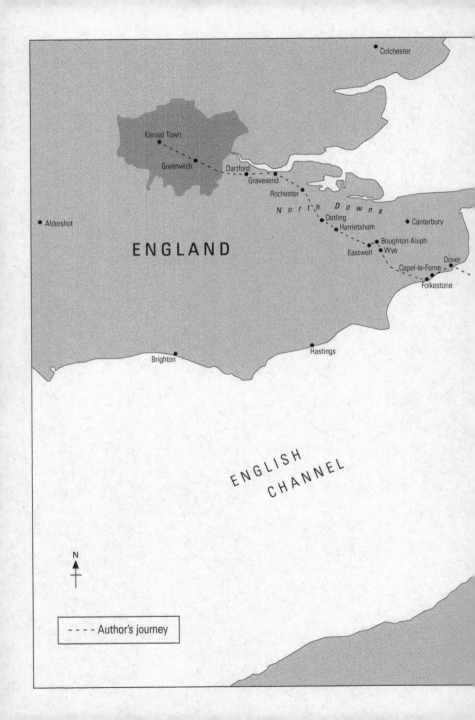

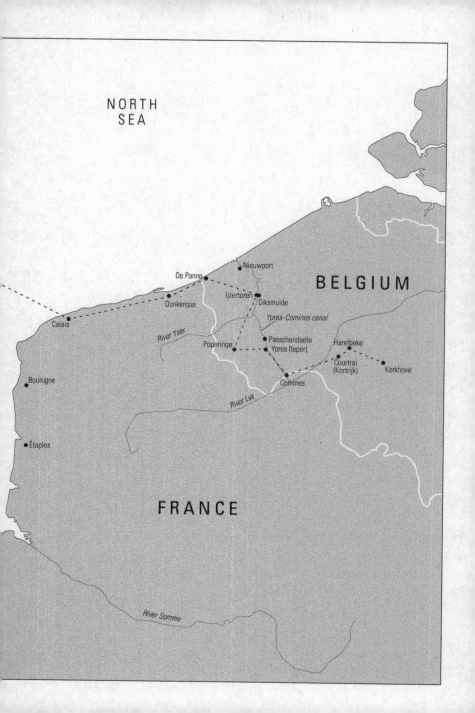

CONTENTS

1

'A SHADOW FLITTING ON THE VERY EDGE OF HISTORY'

I didn't know it at the time but the silence on the other end of the line was the silence of nearly a century.

I'd been researching the family tree and was proving to be barely competent as a beginner genealogist. That said, I'd somehow managed to barge my clumsy way back through the records as far as the beginning of the twentieth century, and I was on the phone to my dad to update him on some of the things I'd found.

'... So, yes, North Kensington was where your grandparents were living at the time, just by Ladbroke Grove,' I said. 'Oh,' I added, almost as an afterthought, 'and I've also found your uncle Edward who was killed in the First World War.'

Silence.

'I didn't know anything about that,' said the quiet voice at the other end of the line.

Private Edward Charles John Connelly of the 10th Battalion, Queen's (Royal West Surrey) Regiment was killed in Flanders on 4 November 1918. He was nineteen years old. Edward was my grandfather's elder brother, my father's uncle, and here was my father telling me that he didn't even know he'd *had* an uncle Edward.

How could it be that my dad, who was given the middle name Edward when he was born more than two decades after Edward Connelly's death, had never been told about his own uncle? Dad had always told me that his father, who was barely sixteen years old when the Great War ended, had lied about his age and enlisted, but never spoke about what he experienced. To think that included the actual existence of his brother, however, seemed an extraordinary thing.

But then, my grandfather's reticence was not unusual. It's something you hear quite often about men of that generation: how the things they saw and experienced had been so traumatising that they'd compartmentalised their memories and sent them away to somewhere in the furthest wispy caverns of the mind, never to emerge again. My grandfather was to all intents and purposes still a child during the war, yet he'd been to a place about as close to hell on earth as anyone could imagine. Is it any wonder that he wasn't chatting amiably away about it at the kitchen table while filling in his pools coupon? Maybe in there, enmeshed among the memories and experiences that he'd closed away for ever, was his own brother who'd gone off to war and never come home. Maybe he'd felt some kind of survivor guilt – that the boy who really had no business being there in the first place had returned but his big brother never did, never had the chance to marry and have a family, to have a long and busy life and leave a legacy of memories and experience that would succeed him for generations.

Maybe this was how Edward Connelly fell between the cracks of history and the fissures of memory to lie forgotten in the Belgian mud for the best part of a century. Perhaps this is how the silence fell over a boy sent off to war, to die in a strange country at the arse-end of a horrendous conflict that was effectively all over, pending official confirmation from a bunch of paunchy bigwigs with fountain pens in a French railway carriage a week later. The mystery of the forgotten soldier in the family history was one that would come to intrigue me more and more.

Of all the pointless deaths of the 1914–18 conflict, Edward Connelly's seems more pointless than most. The war on the Western Front was all but over, and the armies were effectively going through the motions. By 4 November 1918 the outcome was beyond doubt: the Germans had gambled everything on their spring offensive earlier in the year and, despite making significant territorial gains, had been forced back way beyond their original lines and all but collapsed. Morale at home and on the Front had imploded. The money was running out. The game was up. The last couple of weeks before the armistice were pretty much token efforts at attack and defence, largely spent with the Allies chasing the retreating Germans across the Belgian countryside towards Germany.

One of those token efforts killed a token soldier: Private Edward Connelly, a nineteen-year-old railway-carriage washer from West London.

I knew nothing about him or the circumstances of his death, but it all seemed so pointless and unfair and I wanted to know more. I tried to find out as much as I could about Edward Connelly to fill in the uncle-shaped hole in my dad's life, but it soon became clear there really wasn't much to go on. There was a birth certificate dated 25 April 1899. I found a baptism record. He appeared on the censuses for 1901 and 1911 as a two-year-old and a twelve-year-old living in North Kensington in London. There was an entry in 'Soldiers Died in the Great War, 1914–1919' and a record of his grave at the Commonwealth War Graves Commission. And that was it; that was all I could find.

There isn't even a service record for him covering his time in the 10th Queen's. These are often full of extraordinary detail, from the soldier's physical appearance to their medical records and accounts of breaches of discipline and their attendant punishments, but around two thirds of these individual soldier files from the First World War were destroyed during the Blitz. Edward's was one of them. The forgotten soldier was doing a flawless job of being forgotten.

Beyond these scant pieces of information Edward Connelly left nothing behind when he fell in the Flanders mud that cold November day in 1918, and within a generation all those who had known him and could remember him were dead. It was almost as if he died with them a second time.

As time passed I grew more and more uncomfortable about the way Edward had vanished from history. I began to feel ashamed that we didn't know who he was, and angry that his life had been snuffed out in such a pointless way – a week before the armistice, for heaven's sake. Whatever the rights and wrongs of the war itself, at least if he'd died at Passchendaele or the Somme there would be a sense that he had been fighting for something. The date of his death just made things worse: not only had he been forgotten, but his death had been for nothing.

Having rediscovered him, I began to feel responsible for his legacy, or lack of it. I wanted to find out more about his life and how, where and why he died. According to the Commonwealth War Graves Commission he was buried at the Harlebeke New British Cemetery near Courtrai (the French spelling of modern Kortrijk), close to the Franco-Belgian border. What was he doing there? Where had he been? How did a teenager from an Irish immigrant family in the poorest part of North-West London come to be a private in the Queen's (Royal West Surrey) Regiment and die in a futile battle in the final twitching throes of the First World War?

I resolved to find out, but given the dearth of records available I wasn't just beginning from a standing start, I was practically standing on one leg.

For one thing, although I studied history and have written about it for a living, I'd never been remotely interested in war or military history. At school we'd covered the causes of the First World War in our history lessons, but given that I had spent most of them alongside Tim Bennett at the back of the class drawing recreations of the weekend's better First Division goals in our exercise books, not many of those causes actually went in.

One November an elderly maths teacher who had fought in the Second World War addressed our morning assembly on the last Friday before Remembrance Sunday. It was one of the rare occasions that we all listened, as he described how if every British man killed in the First World War marched two by two in through one door of the building and out through the other at regular military marching pace, twenty-four hours a day without break, it would take three weeks for every dead man to pass through. That was something that stuck.

Studying the war poets piqued a little interest. We were handed a collection called *Up the Line to Death*, which made an impression on me in that I could remember some of Wilfred Owen's famous lines, mainly because they struck me as so anti-war in sentiment. I had no idea at the time, of course, but Owen was killed on the same day as my great-uncle, a few miles further south.

I knew names like the Somme, Ypres and Passchendaele but wasn't entirely sure why. I'd laughed at *Blackadder Goes Forth* and been struck dumb by its poignant final scenes. I'd buy a poppy if I saw one and observe the minute's silence in front of the television every Armistice Day, but that was about it.

In Sarajevo I stood on the exact spot from where the Serb nationalist Gavrilo Princip fired the shots into Archduke Franz Ferdinand and his wife Sofia that killed them both and pushed over the first domino in the chain that led to the largest conflict the world had ever seen, and found it strangely underwhelming. I was more interested in the scars left by the most recent Balkan conflict, which were still evident all around the city, from the shrapnel spatters in the plasterwork of just about every building to the red resin Sarajevo Roses in the streets that filled the star-shaped shell scars from the artillery that had rained down on the city during the siege of the early nineties. This had been a war from my lifetime, one I'd seen on news bulletins as it happened. The First World War seemed so distant; there was nothing in Sarajevo to evoke it for me. Even as I stood on the noisy, fumy Bosnian street corner where it had all started, the First World War remained purely one-dimensional, tangential at best to everything in which I was actually interested.

Stumbling inadvertently across my great-uncle Edward changed that. I couldn't stop thinking about him, what he might have been through and about how unfair it was that he'd been entirely forgotten. I found myself feeling angry at the pathetic, pointless waste of a young life, and guilty that he'd been expunged from the family narrative. With the deaths of its last survivors still comparatively recent, it's not long since the First World War passed from memory into history, yet for me it was trying to move in completely the other direction.

I was confused as to why Edward's death might be affecting me more than any of the others that I found in my family research. There were a number of early deaths equally as tragic and untimely: I'm descended from dock workers, with all the attendant accidents and disease that went with that line of work and the way of life that went with it. I had ancestors killed on quaysides and dying young from diseases and medical conditions that are entirely preventable today: my grandmother's tuberculosis, my uncle Eric, who died from gastroenteritis at the age of eight months in the 1930s, surely equally as poignant, equally as tragic?

But Uncle Edward's death in battle came to dominate everything else I'd found. Why should death in combat be any different from other untimely Victorian and Edwardian demise? Why should that be?

War, whether necessary or not, is humanity at its worst. Sometimes it can bring out the best in humanity:

compassion, courage and selflessness, but the unimaginable horrors thrown up by the arrogance of certainty are an awful way to resolve awful situations. I can't bear conflict of any kind. I've not been in a fist fight since a disagreement over a cup of tea with Gary Wayman when I was fourteen, and even then I'm not sure he noticed. Maybe Edward Connelly's death stood out because war is such an alien concept to me, and I was imposing myself on his experience, wondering how I'd have coped, if I'd have coped. The thought of having to create enough hate and aggression to be able to kill a person is a bizarre one – even if it is based on the grounds that if you don't kill them they're probably going to kill you – especially if, like me, you're a yellow-bellied scaredy-cat. And maybe there lies the rub.

When I tried to imagine what he'd been through I was trying to imagine myself in that situation: enlisting, being issued with a uniform, being trained and turned into a weapon of war, travelling out of the country for the first time ever, travelling out of *London* for the first time ever, being thrown into a war that had already been raging for the best part of four years, being among total strangers in a way of life and a daily routine that was completely alien to me, the subsuming of the individual into the whole, the constant threat of imminent, random death from a shell, a gas attack, sniper fire, a machine gun while advancing through no man's land, a bayonet in a trench raid – even drowning in a flooded shell hole.

It was me I was imagining there, not Edward Connelly. It was me I was displacing from a comfortable everyday life of DVD box sets, the corner shop, Charlton Athletic, paying the council tax and eating takeaway noodles in front of *Coronation Street* into the world of mud, trenches, lice, Woodbines, gas masks, artillery shells, bully beef and all-pervading death. My life, my circumstances and my character were not remotely like-for-like comparable with his. Not even close.

The less I knew about Edward the more determined I became to find out. Finding the location of his grave made him slightly less of an enigma. He was out there. There was a headstone with his name on it. There was something tangible of Edward Connelly beyond a scan of a census return on a computer screen. He had left something behind, even if it was just his name chiselled into a piece of Portland stone over a box of his bones in a country that's not his own.

It struck me that it was unlikely to the point of near certainty that anybody had ever visited his grave. He'd lain there in the Belgian soil for nearly a century, alone, forgotten and unvisited, his grave meticulously tended by committed and dedicated strangers to whom he was just a name among names. His background was one of extreme poverty: his parents would never have been able to afford to visit Belgium even if they'd had the opportunity. It might never even have crossed their minds. All his mother had was a devastating telegram, his posthumous campaign medals and her memories. No funeral, no grave to tend, none of the accepted rituals that go with the death of a loved one, and that's even before you consider that no parent should ever have to bury their child.

Edward Connelly is a shadow flitting on the very edge of history. He left behind no letters, no diaries, no poems, no sketches – nothing. There are no anecdotes or testimonies to his character or appearance, no eulogies to the cheekiness of his smile, the twinkle of his eyes, the quickness of his wit, the kindness of his heart. There's no clue as to whether he spent his Saturday afternoons at Queen's Park Rangers or took the bus to Lord's cricket ground. We don't know if he liked a drink, jiggled baby cousins on his knee, argued with his father, brought his mother flowers when he could, tickled his younger siblings until they begged him to stop, kicked a football around the streets with his friends, took my grand-father catching tadpoles by the canal, exalted in the fresh-ness of a spring day, liked to sing songs after a couple of drinks, was perennially late for work, had a sweetheart or paid sixpence at the music halls to hear Vesta Tilley when-ever he could. Was he known as Eddie, or Ted, or Ed, or something else altogether? We'll never know because he's gone. All of him is gone. He's a name written on a handful of official documents and chiselled into a gravestone. Edward Connelly has no legacy.

I have nothing in common with him beyond a surname and the fact that his middle name matches my first name. I don't know why it troubled me so much that my great uncle had been forgotten, why I could still hear that silence on the end of the phone whenever I thought about him. It was the silence that troubled me most, because it seemed it could never be broken.

When it became clear that he really had left nothing behind, my increasing desire to find out more about Edward Connelly forced me to take a different approach, an approach that led to two resolutions. If I couldn't find

Edward's own personal story then I'd try to piece it together in other ways. I'd find other people's stories. I'd seek out letters and diaries of lads like Edward, ordinary young men born at the twilight of a century and thrust into extraordinary circumstances while they were barely coming to terms with adulthood. Lads who never rose through the ranks, who didn't write inspiring stanzas that would fill anthologies for decades to come, who in most cases did nothing special except survive. Lads who would have known the reality of the dugout, the duckboard, the puttee, the mess tin, the endless parade ground drilling, the channel crossing, the glare of the Very light, the whistle of the incoming shell, the banter, the songs, the latrines, the zing of a passing bullet, the ceaseless rain, the cloying mud and the constant presence of death.

I might not get to know Edward Connelly personally, but if I could get to know the lads who were there and left their memories behind then maybe, just maybe, I might know something of Edward Connelly, the life he led and the war he endured and almost survived.

In addition I wanted to make amends, probably to assuage my own wishy-washy feelings of guilt as much as anything. But I sincerely believed that the family owed Edward something for the near century of silence. When I found the Harlebeke New British Cemetery on a map I knew exactly what I had to do. I'd set off to walk from his birthplace in West London and keep walking until I reached his grave in Flanders, making a literal journey through his life and his war. A pilgrimage of sorts, and a penance, I suppose. From my home in London I could board a couple of trains and be at his graveside in barely three hours, but that felt far too easy; he deserved more of an effort than that. If I was going to be Edward's first ever visitor I'd have to put in a bit more work than tapping my card details into the Eurostar website and booking a hotel. By making the journey from his cradle to his grave – on foot, out on the road, free of distraction – I'd have time to think about him and his war: crossing the channel as he did and seeing the horizons he saw, the towns he passed through and, finally, the grave where he lies.

From archive to footpath, I was going in search of Edward Connelly, the forgotten soldier.

2

'THE BOY FROM SOAPSUDS ISLAND'

Edward Connelly was born on 25 April 1899, on the cusp of the twentieth century and in the twilight of the Victorian age. Indeed, as Edward drew his first breath, final tweaks were being made to the plans to mark Queen Victoria's eightieth birthday celebrations: in high streets across the land men sawed and hammered away on massive triumphal arches to be covered in flowers and draped with flags and banners.

Elsewhere, the new, £27,000 Palace Pier in Brighton was undergoing its last lick of paint ahead of its grand opening a few weeks hence. Aston Villa and Liverpool were neck and neck at the top of the Football League as the season entered its final weeks; W.G. Grace was a few weeks away from playing his final Test match.

Joseph Conrad's *Heart of Darkness* had just completed its serialisation in *Blackwood's Magazine*, while Rudyard Kipling had recently published 'The White Man's Burden'. Edward Elgar was putting the final touches to his *Enigma Variations* as Monet was establishing himself on the fifth floor of London's Savoy Hotel, ready to commence his famous series of Thames paintings.

uglielmo Marconi was sending the first radio signals across the English Channel, on the other side of which the messy Dreyfus affair was finally drawing to a close: the much-sinned-against French officer would be out of prison before the century ended. The Boxer Rebellion was prompting endless column inches in British newspapers on the moral failings of the Chinese, while even further away the British Antarctic Expedition was hunkering down for the first ever over-wintering on the continent.

Art, music, exploration, literature, sport, science, imperialism: as the nineteenth century eased towards its close, the themes that had defined it were preparing to push on into its successor. All of this was happening a long way from Gadsden Mews in North Kensington, however, where Edward Charles John Connelly was born to George and Marion Connelly ten months after their marriage the previous year.

Mews properties may sound quite fancy these days, but as London slums went Gadsden Mews was among the worst. It was a small, cramped, overcrowded clutch of dingy tenement buildings squeezed into a tiny space to the rear of other streets of slum housing, the centre of a triangular street pattern that began with the borders of the Great Western Railway to the north, the Grand Union Canal to the south and east and Ladbroke Grove to the west and shrank concentrically to the cramped, claustrophobic dankness of Gadsden Mews. Victorian poverty campaigner Charles Booth noted around the time of Edward's birth that Gadsden Mews was 'very poor looking, dirty, grimy'. The area had grown up rapidly from the 1840s with the coming of the railways and the canal, to become known as one of London's worst slums. So many women worked as laundresses – including Edward's mother and grandmother – that the area became known as 'Soapsuds Island'. Charities including the Protestant missions did their best to alleviate some of the poverty, but it was a losing battle. This was the world into which Edward Connelly, the boy from Soapsuds Island, was born.

In many ways Edward was a product of the century that was ending as he entered it. He came from Irish stock: his great-grandfather John and great-grandmother Catherine had come to London from a small townland outside Youghal in the east of County Cork in 1842. It was just before the Great Famine, but there had been a number of smaller famines at the time and the Connellys were living in a tiny one-room house, trying in vain to live off the land. John, as the eldest, had to leave to make one less mouth to feed. He took advantage of a price war between steam packet companies to find a cheap passage on the crowded deck of a boat that docked at Shadwell in East London some time in 1842, where he and Catherine would live in various tenements for the rest of their lives while John got what work he could 'on the stones' at the docks until his death from tuberculosis in 1890 at the age of sixty-five. The desperate times are no better demonstrated than by the four months' hard labour John did in Newgate Prison in 1852 after he was caught selling watches stolen from the hold of a ship on which he was working.

Around 1890 Edward's father George moved from the East End to the burgeoning North-West London Irish community in search of work on the railways. While living among Irish immigrants in Admiral Place, a stone's throw from the mews in Kensal Town, he courted an English girl living in the same building; they married and the newlyweds took a room in Gadsden Mews as their first marital home.

Marion Christopher, Edward's mother, came from Dorset agricultural stock. The Christophers had lived for many generations in and around Blandford in Dorset, never owning land but always working it. Her parents joined the increasing migration from the uncertainty of the country-side to the greater employment prospects of the cities at the height of the Industrial Revolution, making the long jour-ney from rural Dorset to the tenements of West London in 1874. Marion was the first Christopher to be born among the cramped, dirty streets of North Kensington, in the summer of 1877 to George and Mary Jane Christopher. George had been in the Royal Artillery for a period as a younger man, but on moving to London he found himself getting whatever labouring work he could.

At the time of Edward's birth, Marion's younger brother Robert Christopher had just left for the Boer War as a soldier with the 2nd Battalion of the Queen's (Royal West Surrey) Regiment, the same regiment that Edward would join eight-een years later. Robert had enlisted the previous year at the age of seventeen and would spend three years fighting in South Africa before being wounded and sent home to England in 1902. When the First World War broke out he was labouring in a power station, but his previous military career led to him being recalled to the army as a private in the 6th Battalion of the Queen's (Royal West Surrey)

Regiment. Robert Christopher died of wounds sustained in a raid on German positions at the Hohenzollern Redoubt near Bethune on 5 April 1916.

Born to Irish immigrants on one side and refugees of the Industrial Revolution on the other, Edward was an archetype of the late-nineteenth-century urban working class. His and their worlds were small, their horizons narrow: both families lived for more than half a century within the same tiny network of streets in North-West London. It was from there that I would set off on my journey to find the forgotten soldier.

3

'A LONG, HARD JOURNEY
THROUGH A SHORT, HARD LIFE'

One hundred and fifteen years after his birth, almost to the day, Edward Connelly's locality looked quite different to the one he knew, especially on one of those spring mornings that make even the Harrow Road happy. There was the cheeriness of renewal everywhere – a freshness in the air; even the rattling rasp of the grilles going up at the bookmakers and money-transfer shops seemed to have a tangible jauntiness. The half-dozen people waiting for the post office to open smiled and chatted. Two men in bright-blue overalls with the legend 'Love the Town You Live In' written on the back of their hi-vis vests rumbled by, wheeling a bin full of brushes. As the sun climbed higher into the sky and forced the shadows into retreat towards the shop fronts, a young woman wearing a puffa jacket waiting in the post-office queue put her head back, closed her eyes and smiled to herself as the sunshine warmed her face. The sky was deep blue and cloudless, bare save for the swollen ghost of an aircraft contrail.

I ordered a cup of tea in a café, sat down at a Formica table, reached into my bag and pulled out a dog-eared copy of the *London A–Z* along with a folded map: a reproduction of an Ordnance Survey of the area from 1913. I found the right page of the A–Z and opened the old map, placing them side by side on the table, two landscapes divided by a century but whose urban contours made them recognisable as the same place. I ran my forefinger down the page of the A–Z and then did the same to the map until I found where I needed to go.

On the old map, Gadsden Mews is there in the east of Kensal Town, a wedge of North-West London still hemmed in today by the canal, the railway and Ladbroke Grove. Within this triangle on the old map, concentric streets of tightly packed houses shrink towards the very centre where, shoehorned into a cramped space between the backs of the residences, there are two rows of tiny squares named Gadsden Mews. There's no Gadsden Mews on the A–Z, it's long gone, but the surrounding streets survive and I could at least get close if I could find Hazelwood Crescent.

I drank my tea, headed back out into the sunshine, turned east along the Harrow Road, crossed the bridge over the canal and walked towards where Gadsden Mews used to be.

After crossing the canal I headed for the landmark of Erno Goldfinger's Trellick Tower until I found Hazelwood Crescent nestling in its considerable shadow. The entrance to Gadsden Mews had been at a slight dog-leg kink in Hazelwood Crescent that's still there today, so I'd be able to pinpoint almost exactly where the mews once lay. The streets were quiet as I reached the hint of a bend I was looking for. On this spot had been the only way in and out of the slum tenements, the tiny three-storey wooden houses packed with the poorest of the poor, where whole families often lived in single rooms with little in the way of comfort or sanitation. Kensal Town itself was a poor area, but even Kensal Towners would probably have looked down on Gadsden Mews.

I gauged my bearings and stood for a moment looking into where the entrance used to be. Ahead of me was Hazelwood Tower and to my right was the gable end of a low block of flats. I was about to move on when the sign on the front of the block of flats caught my eye – it was called Gadsden House. So there *was* an echo of the old place here after all. I walked around a little further, passed between a couple of apartment blocks and made my way into the centre of the Kensal New Town estate at the heart of which was a tarmacked basketball court bordered by a bright blue metal cage where the breeze moved a few leaves around in a far corner. The gate was open; I walked onto the court and stood at its centre. Hazelwood Tower dominated one end and on one side the court was overlooked by the balconies of Gadsden House. Somewhere beneath my feet lay the heart of Gadsden Mews. Somewhere here, within no more than a few feet of where I stood and where my shadow fell, was where my great-grandparents had eked out their lives of relentless hardship and poverty, and where Edward Connelly was born.

Ahead of me lay a long, hard journey through a short, hard life. Around 175 miles south-east of me, as the crow flies, was a small, neat, unvisited grave. I looked a little incongruous standing in the middle of an empty public basketball court on an estate in North-West London clad in full walking gear and rucksack, but this was where a story with a mysterious, tragic ending began. I was beginning my physical journey from the cradle to the grave, through the all-too-brief life of Edward Connelly. I took a last look around, shifted my rucksack into a more comfortable position, strode away from the basketball court and set out for Belgium.

4

'A HALF-DEAF KID FROM THE SLUMS OF KENSAL TOWN'

It would be more than a year before Edward was christened, perhaps suggesting he was a sickly baby for whom the first year was touch and go. But he survived and by 1901 the family had moved from Gadsden Mews to Admiral Mews, a few hundred yards west, close to the railway lines. It doesn't seem as if they were moving up in the world. Booth's notebooks, having set out the extreme poverty of the surrounding streets, described Admiral Mews as: 'If anything worse than the foregoing. Houses on north side only and a few stables at the eastern and western extremities. Rough, noisy, all doors open, passages and stairs all bare boards, the usual mess … Gipsy looking women standing about, Irish. The worst of this block of streets.'

Two-year-old Edward was no longer living with his parents. Instead he was living with his grandparents, which was probably more to do with the nature of the tenements than any family disagreements. They were living in the same building, but George and Marion were in one room with Robert, my grandfather, aged eight, while Marion's parents, the Christophers, George and Mary-Ann, lived with Edward in two rooms along with their 42-year-old son John.

Edward received some rudimentary schooling at the local mission school, but for families like the Connellys the capacity to supplement the meagre household income was always the priority, and Edward would have been sent out to work as early as possible, probably at the age of fourteen. In the 1911 census, when he was twelve, he was still living with his grandparents and his uncle John in Admiral Mews, close to his parents, but there's one extra detail: on the census return Edward is described as 'a bit deaf'.

Within weeks of that census John Christopher died suddenly at home from a brain haemorrhage. It's very possible Edward was there as his uncle held his head, let out an agonised cry and lurched across the room, scattering furniture and belongings before crashing to the floor in the corner, limp, motionless and ash-grey.

Edward next turns up in the 1915 wage books of the Great Western Railway's Old Oak Common railway depot, a vast establishment that employed a large number of local men and boys. Edward's job was washing railway carriages, not a pleasant task in the age of steam and unchecked industrial pollution. He'd finish his shifts grimy and black with soot and filth, exhausted and arm-sore from the relentless brushing, but he was bringing in an income, which for a half-deaf kid from the slums of Kensal Town was about all that could be asked of him.

It's after this that the trail goes cold until Edward's death. He would have been fifteen years old when war broke out in the summer of 1914, but it's impossible to know what kind of impact it would have had on him and life in Kensal Town. His uncle Robert would have gone off to fight almost immediately, but we can only guess at how this might have affected Edward. Were they close? Robert lived in the same warren of streets, so he would probably have been a regular visitor to his sister and grandparents. Edward would have seen his uncle frequently as he grew up, but what would his thoughts have been about the war? How would he have taken the news of his uncle's death in 1916? Would he have expected to go? Would he have tried to enlist under-age? What was the nature of discussion among his friends and neighbours? The talk around Admiral Mews – of enlistment, of the men who had already gone, of the prospects for a quick resolution to the conflict – would have been replicated in every street and among every boy of Edward's generation. There hadn't been an event in history at that point to unite a nation and affect its everyday life like the First World War. It permeated every county, every town, every street and every home. Nobody was unaffected.

Most of us will have an Edward Connelly in our backgrounds: a youngster born on the cusp of centuries who'd grow up to be a participant, willing or not, in the greatest war and the greatest tragedy of the modern age up until then. These lads weren't poets, they weren't officer material – they did nothing heroic beyond their best. They went off to war as cheerily as they could, made the best of it, had no say in its strategy or planning and just did what they were told. Many of them came home afterwards and resumed their lives; others didn't and lie to this day in the soil of France, Belgium and further afield. These lads were raised among grimy cobbles rather than the playing fields of Eton, and there were thousands of them right across the land.

Take Admiral Terrace, for example, where the Connellys and the Christophers lived. According to the 1911 census there were twenty-nine households in Admiral Terrace containing 127 people of all ages, from elderly couples to enormous family broods crammed into the pokey rooms of eleven shabby buildings. I combed through these records for the names of men and boys who would have been of official military age during the First World War and then compared those names to any surviving military records I could find. I unearthed eight men, not including Edward, who went off to war, four of whom were killed. Two of those who died were brothers: William and John Lovell, twenty and twenty-three respectively, killed in March and August 1918. Including Edward, that's five First World War deaths from one small North London street of eleven properties. Bear in mind how most soldiers' records from the Great War were destroyed during the Blitz: these are just what I could find in the surviving files.

The war came to visit every street and practically every building. Everyone had a son, a father, a nephew, a godson, a son-in-law, a brother, a cousin at the Front. We all have grandfathers, great-grandfathers, even great-great-grandfathers who served, in addition to the attendant generational strata of uncles. Ordinary men, not heroes; men of whom there's little of note: they didn't win medals beyond the campaign ones that everyone received; they weren't court-martialled; there's no specific record of any acts of heroism; they were never promoted beyond the rank of private, and they didn't expect to be. They just turned up, did their duty as best they could, smoked their cigarettes, drank their rum ration and tried to get through it.

Edward's story isn't unique. It's the story of many, the story that's in your family background as well as mine. Edward is an everyman, his experiences similar to thousands upon thousands of others who left nothing behind, no letters, no diaries, no poems. Yet some of them did leave stories behind. In order to fill in the yawning gaps in Edward's life and war, it was time to unearth the narratives of his contemporaries, to construct the tale of all the ordinary men in the poor bloody infantry in the name of Edward Connelly. The forgotten soldier, anonymous for the best part of a century, would stand up from the decades of silence and shout on behalf of all the men like him.

I delved into archives, read yellowing letters and leafed through diaries, struggled through regimental histories and watched hours of documentaries. I listened to old recordings made years after the war, old men's voices from broad Geordie to lilting Sussex burr, occasionally punctuated in the background by the chimes of a mantelpiece clock marking another hour passed since the horror of the trenches. Dead men's voices now, but in my headphones they were alive, animated, chuckling, emotional, tentative, sad and forthright. Making sure that we would remember as they transported themselves in their minds from silent sitting rooms of china ornaments and antimacassars back to the mud, noise, fear and death of the Western Front. These men had seen what Edward had seen, heard what Edward had heard, feared what Edward had feared, yet they were able to tell their stories and make sure that they could still be told long after their own deaths – and longer still after the events they described.

I'd come to know well men like George Fortune, Fred Dixon, William Dann and the rest in my quest for the life of Edward Connelly and all the other forgotten soldiers.

5

'I WAS AT LUNCH ON THIS PARTICULAR DAY AND THOUGHT, I SUPPOSE I'D BETTER GO AND JOIN THE ARMY'

When war was declared the British Army had just under 250,000 officers and men. They were backed up by just over 300,000 territorials and around 230,000 conventional reservists.

The British Expeditionary Force under Field Marshal Sir John French that crossed the Channel in August 1914 consisted of 81,000 men, including two cavalry divisions. It was, of course, all supposed to be over by Christmas, but by October the first trenches had been dug and four years of attrition on the Western Front were under way. When Christmas arrived there were nearly 270,000 British troops in France and Belgium. By the time of the German Spring Offensive of 1918, the front line, twelve miles long in the autumn of 1914, stretched from the North Sea coast to the Swiss border.

Once the stalemate had been established Lord Kitchener estimated that it could take up to three years to overcome the Germans, a lengthy war for which the British Army was utterly underprepared. He began vigorous campaigns to encourage recruitment in order to build an entire new army. In fact, there would be five Kitchener Armies, mostly comprising six divisions of twelve battalions each.

The initial reaction among the men of Britain was rampant enthusiasm: for one thing, early enlisters were generally able to choose their regiment, hence they could remain with their friends and colleagues, and for another, the wave of patriotism in the light of Blighty going to war washed thousands through the doors of the recruiting offices. Everything was done to encourage men to enlist, from poster campaigns to the creation of the 'pals battalions', which were raised in the belief that if groups of men from certain towns or professions could stick together the chances of mass recruitment would be greater. They were right, too: in Lancashire, for example, the Accrington Pals Battalion reached 1,000 recruits in just ten days. The intention might have been admirable, but when entire pals battalions were being all but wiped out (of the 720 Accrington Pals at the first day of the Battle of the Somme, 584 were either killed, wounded or never seen again) it was leaving huge, irreplaceable holes in communities, and the idea was soon dropped.

At first, the enlistment procedure was fairly rigorous compared to how much it would relax later: you had to be between the ages of nineteen and thirty-eight, at least five foot three inches in height and have a reasonable level of fitness. If Edward had tried to join up under-age early in the war it's likely his partial deafness would have seen him turned away.

The process was straightforward: each recruit was given a brief interview and filled out an attestation form which, when signed by both the recruiting officer and the recruit, committed the latter to serve in the army for the duration of the war. He then swore an oath of allegiance before an officer, underwent a medical examination, another officer countersigned his approval and the man was officially a 'Soldier subject to the King's Regulation'. He was given a shilling (the famous king's shilling) and either handed a railway pass to a training camp or told to go home and await the call-up to begin his training.

George Fortune, born in Dover in February 1899 and the son of a diver at Dover Harbour, was six weeks older than Edward.

'My father used to say that a man who goes into the army is not fit for anything else,' he recalled. '"Once a soldier, never a man," that's what he said.'

George's father, also called George, worked from 6 a.m. to 6 p.m. and walked three miles to work every day, and then three miles home in the evening. According to George the only time his father would take the tram was if he'd been bell diving and come up with the bends. He was a tough, taciturn man and he was tough on his son.

'I think he was a bit disappointed in me,' George recalled. 'He would say, "Give him another basin of sop, we will never rear him."'

George's grandmother on his mother's side was Annie Ovenden from Cork in the south of Ireland, the same part of the country from which Edward's family had come. His father's family also had Irish roots and George liked to think of himself as Irish. He was very close to his grandmother and would visit her whenever he could.

'I used to go straight from school and she'd be waiting at her gate,' he said. 'She used to cuddle me up to her and always smelt of snuff and peppermint. Sometimes she used to send me to the pub to get a gill of gin for sixpence: I knew then that Father Laws was coming to see her.'

Although his mother left his father when George was five years old, and his father didn't seem like the warmest of men, George appears to have had a happy childhood. As youngsters he and his friends would play and bathe by Shakespeare's Cliff.

'The trains used to come through the tunnel there from Folkestone', he recalled. 'When we heard a train coming, we used to come out of the water and dance, and the old ladies would pull down the blinds.'

Young George even witnessed, practically on his door-step, one of the great moments from history when, one morning in 1908, he and his brother Walter got up early, walked to North Fallen and watched Louis Blériot make a bumpy landing to complete the first air crossing of the English Channel.

Dover has always been an important place geographically and strategically. The imposing castle still overlooks the town and George was always keenly aware of the military, especially the Navy. The Fortunes lived at Clarendon Place in a working-class area in the west of the town, and one of their neighbours was a naval seaman.

'Whenever he came home on leave he set the street alight. He would hire a barrel organ in town and park it outside his house. He would have everybody dancing and singing,' said George.

Soldiers had been a common sight in the streets of Dover since before the Napoleonic Wars, and they were equally visible during the first decade of the twentieth century. One hot day George was drinking from a horse trough on the Folkestone Road when a horse galloped up and arrived next to him.

'I saw a bundle of khaki on the ground hanging from a stirrup,' George recalled. 'It was a soldier who had been thrown from his horse and dragged about a mile.'

It wasn't all hapless horsemen and innocent mischief, though. On his way home from the cliffs one day George came across the body of a soldier with his throat cut. The boys raised the alarm, but not before George secured himself a souvenir.

'I took his hat,' said George. 'He was in the Buffs [the Royal East Kent Regiment] and I played soldiers with it. My brother Walter told my dad I'd pinched the soldier's hat but all he said was, "Well, he won't be needing it any more."'

Things changed for George a year or so before war broke out when his father was badly injured at work. Going to school one day he'd seen George senior on a tram and, given the time of day and the fact that his father was proud of how he walked everywhere, he knew immediately something was wrong.

'He was sitting, leaning forward,' George recalled. 'He'd had an accident and broken some ribs. There were always accidents and people killed at the harbour. It was dangerous work. He never went back to work at the harbour and I don't think he got a penny from them.'

George was sent to live with his grandmother while his father recovered. When George senior was well enough he found a job at the local convent repairing boots for fifteen shillings a week. Meanwhile, having been rejected by the navy because his chest measured an inch below the minimum, Walter, whom George looked up to like a hero, joined the army.

Times were hard for the Fortunes and George left school at fourteen for a job as a lather boy at a local barber's shop. For his 3/6 a week George worked from 8 a.m. to 8 p.m., Monday to Friday, and then 8 a.m. to midnight on Saturdays. As well as the lathering, he had to clean the windows, sweep up the hair, clean the copper urns in which the barber heated the water and he even had to clean the boots of the barber's entire family. He was harshly treated, certainly in today's terms, but this elicited little sympathy from the elder Fortune: 'The barber was a little man, about five feet tall, half German, and he was horrible to me. I told Dad about him swearing at me and he said, "It will do you good; you need someone to wake you up."'

When the war came in August 1914, the talk among the young men of Dover was all of joining up and fighting the Hun. Fuelled by boyish bravado the talk might have been, but George's friends soon began disappearing to training camps and then to the Front. Still only fifteen years old, George tried to enlist: 'All the lads were joining up so I tried and said I was nineteen. I was a big boy but I failed the doctor, who said I had a hernia.'

The army doctor referred him to the local hospital for an operation to the remove the hernia, but when he arrived

George found the place overrun with wounded men from the Front brought home by ship from Dunkirk. Reluctant to go under the knife, the youngster instead set about making himself useful.

'The hospital was full and I helped the nurses,' recalled George. 'I was in there three weeks and they forgot who I was: I was like a hospital orderly. I had a fine old lark with the wounded men. I used to jump right over their beds for a bit of fun. Then one day the house surgeon was walking round. He saw me and said, "What's this fellow doing here?" I told him and he said, "Right, we'll have him on the table."'

After the operation George was flat out for ten days, in constant pain. No one visited him except a priest, and when he was well enough to leave he had to walk the mile and a half home. Soon afterwards his sister Cecilia, aware of the fractured nature of the Fortune family in Dover since their father's accident and mother's departure, took him to London while he recuperated from the operation and found him work with her plumber husband in West Hampstead.

'Ciss was a godsend to me,' he remembered. 'I was ill and she brought me back to health. Then I went to work as a plumber's mate and I loved the work.'

This fledgling apprenticeship was brought to an end all too soon, however, when George's brother-in-law joined up and went off to war. George moved on to Highgate to live with his mother and found a job on the Underground. Once settled he wrote to his father but never received a reply – he found out later that his father had emigrated to Australia, taking one of his younger brothers with him. George never saw either of them again.

By 1916 George was working as a gateman at Hammersmith Underground station and living with another older sister, Gladys, whose husband was also away at the Front. Feeling a little like an imposition as Gladys brought up two children in cramped conditions, George decided it was time to try to enlist again and attended the recruiting office at White City: 'The doctor hardly looked at me this time and I was passed A1. I told the railway and they said they couldn't keep the job open for me. I didn't worry much as I was going to be a soldier.'

William Dann, also born in 1899, a couple of months later than Edward, lived along the coast from George in Brighton and would go on to join the same battalion as Edward, the 10th Queen's (Royal West Surrey). Descended from a long line of Sussex agricultural labourers, William bucked the family trend when he left school at fourteen to be apprentice to a painter named Fisher, who employed him to assist in the painting of brewery vans in red, black and gold-leaf livery. It wasn't long before the war impacted on William, too.

'He was a very nice man indeed,' recalled Dann of Fisher. 'But as a reservist in the Royal Marines he was called up almost immediately, and we heard he was killed about three months later.'

Like George, all the talk around him was of the war. The army had sergeants walking around Brighton stopping men apparently of military age and asking them pointedly why they hadn't joined up. One day in 1916 one of them stopped William and, despite being barely seventeen, he decided to go and enlist.

'I was at lunch on this particular day and thought, I suppose I'd better go and join the army, then,' he remembered. 'So I went to the drill hall in Church Street in Brighton, queued up past the sergeant and the policeman on the door and eventually came around to the officers and the sergeant at the recruiting desk. They said, "How old are you?" I said, "Seventeen." "Ooh, no," they said, "that won't do; come back when you're nineteen." As I was going out, the sergeant on the door said, "What? You back already?" I said, "It's no good. They won't take me." He asked why and I said, "I told them my age, seventeen." He looked from side to side, lowered his voice and said, "Well, go and join the queue again and when you get to the front again just say you're nineteen." So that's what I did. Next thing I was sent along to the barracks in Lewes Road for a fitness examination. I came out with an A1 and I was in the army.'

In West Yorkshire, Horace Calvert was another young working-class boy like Edward trying to make his way in the world. Horace was born in September 1899 in Manningham, Bradford, to a father who worked as an assistant to Horace's grandfather at an ironmongery business on Carlisle Road. Horace was one of six children, four girls and two boys.

'It was just the usual everyday life of that time,' said Horace of his childhood. 'I started going out delivering papers and running errands at the age of nine or ten, anything to get some extra money because there were eight of us in the family and money was tight.'

The Calverts lived in a typical northern working-class back-to-back house. It had a parlour, cellar, kitchen, two bedrooms and an attic pressed into service as a bedroom.

There was no hot water, the lighting was gas powered and the toilet was outside, but Horace certainly didn't feel he had a deprived upbringing.

'There was plenty to eat because it was drilled into me by my mother to always make sure you had a roof over your head, warmth in the house and food on the table,' Horace said. 'I don't know how she did it but we had meat every Sunday, which lasted till Monday. We managed all right. Clothing was patched hand-me-downs but on Sunday you were always well turned out as far as possible.'

Like his siblings, Horace was sent to Drummond Road School, where he received a basic education that was fairly typical of the times: 'It was a big school and we were well looked after by the teachers, who were very nice. I learned the three Rs, a little history and we were given talks about behaviour after school hours. We had a concert once a year for the parents.'

At the age of twelve the need to bring some money into the household meant that Horace stopped going to school full time and took a part-time job at Field's Mill in the spinning department. He'd start at 7 a.m., finish at midday, go home for lunch and then spend the afternoon at school. All his wages went into the household, other than the sixpence he was given every Saturday.

'I'd buy little toys, pea-shooters, catapults, a bow and arrow,' he recalled. 'I had plenty of mates and five or six of us would all go to the local park, but you had to be back for bed by 9 o'clock.'

At fourteen Horace went to work full time in a small engineering shop on Richmond Road in Bradford. His father had wanted Horace to learn a trade and wasn't keen on him staying on at the mill doing simple manual work as a full-time occupation.

'The first thing I had to do when I got there in the morning was turn on the gas engine. I didn't like doing that. Then I used to go to a place called Slingsby's, where they made handcarts for warehouses. I had to go and collect the wheels, put them on the boring machine and bore them out ready for fitting on the axle and deliver them back to the firm. Also, I had to take out all the filings from the lathes which were then sold as scrap. I kept the floor clean and would go and watch a chap working the machine to see how it was done: it was a good place for training but after twelve months of this I didn't like it any more. I think it was the dirt and the noise and the running about you had to do. Also, I was on 7 shillings a week; the average wage for a skilled engineer was about 23 shillings.'

Horace, like his contemporaries Edward, George and William, was fifteen when the war broke out, and he remembered it vividly.

'My father told me there could be trouble among nations because we were being warned in the *Telegraph* and the *Argus* about what was happening with Germany,' he said. 'The territorials were actively recruiting even before the war broke out so the authorities must have been expecting something. I was interested in the military because we had a quartermaster sergeant in the territorials living near us and I would see him in his scarlet uniform. Also, our headmaster at school, Lodge was his name, was a sergeant in the TA. In addition, I had a friend whose father was in the artillery, so there was always a little link between me and the military. Believe it or not, in those days before the war if people joined the army you thought they either didn't want to work or they'd got a girl into trouble.'

On 4 August, Horace was up early and on his way to work as usual. When he reached the top of Richmond Road he saw a billboard outside the newsagent announcing in stark black letters 'WAR DECLARED ON GERMANY'.

'Even on that day the military was stopping all the horse-drawn vehicles and examining the horses before taking some of them away,' he said. 'People welcomed the war in the sense that a challenge had been thrown down over Belgium and they were eager to take up that challenge. That first evening a crowd gathered outside the Belle Vue Barracks and they were cheering every time one of the territorials came out. People were singing 'Rule, Britannia!' and all the old favourites outside the barracks. I got so carried away with it all that I stayed there till half-past ten, and I was supposed to be home at nine.'

There hadn't been scenes like it since Bradford City brought home the FA Cup in 1911. In those early days of the fledgling war, when everything seemed so glamorous and easy, Horace watched the men queuing at the recruitment office at the ice rink near his home on Manningham Lane and was already thinking of joining them. The Bradford Pals had just formed, the rink was their headquarters and Horace liked what he saw (2,000 of the Bradford Pals, incidentally, would be at the Somme and 1,770 of them would be killed or wounded on the first day). Bradford was on a war footing and Horace was up for the fight. Every night when he

finished work he'd go to the nearby barracks and glean the
latest information from the sentries about the war and all
the new recruits until he could contain himself no longer.

'I was fifteen when I decided to join up. One morning
instead of going to work I left my working clothes in the
scullery head, went out in my better clothing, walked into
the barracks, lined up, the doctor looked at me, I received
the King's Shilling and that was it, all done inside an hour.
They never questioned my age – I just said I was eighteen
and that was it. I looked at it as a big adventure: I'd read all
the stories in the *Wide World* magazines in the library and it
made me want an adventurous life, so I thought this might
be more exciting than the alternatives. Otherwise life was
just work and a penny to go in the bioscope at the fairground
every now and then. I wanted more than that.'

Horace's enlistment received a mixed reaction at home.
As soon as he walked through the door his father, who'd
seen Horace's work clothes hanging up in the scullery,
demanded to know where he'd been. Horace informed him
he'd just joined the army. There was a pause and his father
said, 'Well, you've made your bed.'

'There were tears from my mother and she said I shouldn't
have done it,' recalled Horace, 'but that was it; it was done.
I told them not to get me out because of my age or I'd just
go somewhere else, like the navy.'

Horace Calvert was going to war.

Fred Dixon came from a slightly less impoverished background near Dorking in Surrey. His father was a draper,
although he would die in 1909 when Fred was just thirteen.
Born in 1896, he was a little older than my great-uncle in

that he was eighteen when he joined up in 1914, but he would come to fight alongside Edward in the 10th Queen's Royal West Surreys later in the war.

His father's death had put paid to Fred's hopes of earning a scholarship to Dorking High School and instead he had to leave at fourteen to become an apprentice to a hosier. Fred didn't take to hosiery and before long secured a job on the bottom rung of the ladder in the stationery trade. 'It was rather Dickensian,' he recalled later. 'I worked more than 60 hours a week for 5 shillings. I didn't have a great deal of leisure time either: on Wednesdays, which was supposed to be my half day, I frequently had to catch an early morning train to London to collect special orders and wouldn't get back until 4:30.'

Despite this demanding work schedule, Fred was able to obtain some basic military training long before the onset of the war, thanks to the lads' brigade at his local church in Woking. Three times a week he'd walk to the drill hall and learn some basic military skills, and received a medal for his aptitude with a bayonet.

The training and drilling sessions always commenced with a hymn, the highly appropriate "Fight the Good Fight", with the curate and captain of the lads' company Reverend Bates at the harmonium.

'He was over 6'3" and sat at this little harmonium pedalling away, looking as if his knees were under his chin, and we'd all sing lustily,' recalled Fred. 'He joined up and later on helped in the forming of Talbot House in Poperinge with Tubby Clayton, which became very famous. He was wounded soon after he got there by a bomb dropped from a German plane over the square, a wound in the foot that ultimately shortened his leg. The bomb killed a girl who was there at the time, too. Tubby Clayton ran over and bandaged his foot for him. Reverend Bates came back from the war, eventually became Canon of Leicester Cathedral and was a very fine man.'

One skill instilled in Fred by Reverend Bates was signalling, which would come to feature very strongly in Fred's time with the 10th Queen's. He also learned gymnastics and map reading, and there would be occasional night operations on local commons. They even had a field gun.

'We used an old muzzle-loading naval gun, with drag ropes like you see on the Royal Tournament on television,' said Fred. 'Teamwork was the essence of the exercise as the gun had little value except for display. It was fired on the odd rare occasion, but the last time the gun was taken out onto Horsham Common it was sponged, failed, rammed and then fired again, but it seems the lad who was sponging the barrel got rather excited and didn't do it properly. When the next charge went in, it was accidentally lit by a spark remaining in the barrel and blew the ramrod out, followed by the hand of the lad who'd been doing the ramming. It probably saved his life when you think about it because the majority of the chaps on the common that day lost their lives during the war. The fellow who lost his hand went on to become the church verger.'

This basic military experience led to Fred becoming among the first to volunteer, enlisting at the end of October 1914 to join a cavalry regiment, something that fulfilled a long-held ambition for him.

'When I was around four years old, the Surrey Yeomanry had a camp on Ranmore Common, on the North Downs between Westcote and Ranmore,' he recalled. 'My mother took me down on a mail cart on the Sunday after they set up camp to see the yeomen. Everything was in apple-pie order when we got there, and it made a deep impression on me seeing these lovely horses and the yeomen walking about in their spurs and riding breeches and uniforms with red facing on the front. Every year after that they'd come through Westcote. My father had a shop on the main road, and I'd stand outside and watch these lovely animals with their shining coats and the men with their spurs, so when the war came it was natural that I'd go into the Surrey Yeomanry, even though I'd never actually ridden a horse.'

At that early stage, however, the ordinary men of England were already seeing through the veneer of cheery optimism that pervaded the posters and propaganda.

'All over by Christmas, they said. I didn't believe that, not a bit of it,' recalled Fred. 'I said to my mother – and I was only eighteen at the time and a young eighteen at that – this affair isn't going to be over by Christmas. They'll have to bring conscription in and I'd sooner volunteer for a regiment of my choice than be conscripted to one I hadn't chosen. She thought I was quite right. That's what I did, and I was very glad I did, too.'

Like Edward, Walter Cook was from North London. Born in June 1899, a few weeks after my great-uncle, in Finsbury Park, Walter would go on to become a stretcher-bearer and medical orderly on the Western Front. His father was an electrician and gas fitter, and Walter had five brothers. It wasn't long till he found his vocation.

'When I was ten I joined a local Boy Scouts unit and found the first-aid work particularly interesting,' he said. 'I managed to get a certificate for it, much to my parents' amazement.'

Blighted by poor eyesight, Walter left school at twelve, even though he wasn't really supposed to: 'They didn't bother with me much. My parents knew the local school inspector well and he liked a drop of the parsnip wine my mother made. One day he came round and it was agreed I'd be better off finding odd jobs than going to school.'

Also like Edward, Walter had a family connection to the military, and the Boer War in particular. His mother's brother was a regular soldier who'd fought in South Africa and would occasionally visit and entertain the Cook brood with tales of his exploits and adventures. When the First World War was declared, Walter's uncle Robert was one of the first to go.

'When the war started he did pay a visit, and I heard him say he was hoping to go to France very shortly,' Walter remembered. 'We liked him, us kids. He drew sketches for us and always seemed to have a joke or a funny story at his fingertips.'

Once he'd left for the front, the Cooks heard little of Robert until January 1915, when he came home wounded and a changed man: 'He came back with a limp and we learned that many of his men of his men who'd been wounded had to be left lying where they were. It was the retreat from Mons, where there'd been many casualties and not nearly enough stretcher-bearers. The fighting had been so fierce and the guns so lethal that going back for the wounded was almost out of the question. He was very glum, thinking about the men they'd had to leave behind for want of a stretcher. That caused me to think a little. That night I went to bed and thought that knowing a bit about first aid I might be able to enlist and help – if I could get past the recruiting officer.'

The next day Walter presented himself at the church in Tollington Park, where he'd once been a choirboy, whose hall now served as the local recruiting office. He joined a long queue of volunteers and, producing his first-aid certificate from his time in the Scouts, declared his intention to join the medical service – while also adding the small matter of two and a half fictional years to his age.

'The doctor quizzed me in a manner that made it clear he doubted my age,' he said. 'But my desire to go and help those fellows lying wounded on the ground was so great I considered it a risk worth taking. I pulled it off and was assigned to an ambulance unit. I didn't tell my family until I'd joined up. They'd always known that if I made up my mind I'd carry it through, so they knew there was little point in protesting.'

I have no way of knowing exactly when Edward enlisted, or even whether he was conscripted, as his records are among those lost in the Blitz. He turned eighteen in April 1917 and might have tried then. He might have tried earlier, like the rest of the lads already mentioned, but been turned down for whatever reason, possibly the deafness cited on the 1911 census.

He might have waited to be conscripted. For all the razzmatazz and rush to enlist in the early years of the war, once word filtered back of the terrible things happening and the enormous numbers of dead, the recruitment of volunteers began to tail off. In August 1915 a national register was taken, a sort of supplementary census, to give the government an idea of just how many men of military age were in the country, and of those how many were fit and willing to volunteer. The results were not particularly encouraging. In January 1916 the Prime Minister, Herbert Asquith, proposed the Military Service Act, in which unmarried men or widowers aged between eighteen and forty-one without children or dependents (the act immediately became known as the 'Bachelors' Bill') would be required to join the fight. It wasn't an immediate success: in the first two months, a quarter of the nigh-on 200,000 men who had been sent call-up papers simply failed to show up. Serving soldiers were sent to large gatherings, like football matches and busy railway stations, to buttonhole men apparently of military age in the crowds and find out whether they'd been avoiding the call. Even with these measures, in May it was deemed necessary to extend the bill to apply to all men between eighteen and forty-one, married, single, widowed, whatever. Later in the war, the high number of casualties and the need for new recruits was so great that in February 1918 the upper age limit was raised to fifty, and the law specifying that a recruit could not actually participate in the war until he turned nineteen was relaxed.

It may have been Edward's youth and deafness that kept him from the front earlier if, as I suspect, he didn't see action until the spring of 1918. The medical examinations varied in their rigorousness at different points of the war. In the early days the doctors were paid a shilling for every man passed but received nothing for a man deemed unfit for service, so the temptation to err on the side of enlistment must have been great. Under conscription, however, the doctors were paid a flat rate and a three-tiered system of fitness was introduced. An A grade meant a man was fit for general service, B meant he was fit for service abroad but in a support capacity, while C designated a man fit for service at home only. Each category was then given a grade between one and three, one being the strongest. By the end of 1916 this system meant that only 6.5 per cent of new recruits were rejected as completely unfit for service, but as the war went on, and the need for more and more troops grew, a greater laxness crept into the system. When murmurs of public disquiet began about the apparent weakness of some of the troops being packed off to the Front, things were tightened up again in 1917.

If the accounts in this chapter are anything to go by, Edward would have been keen to sign up. For one thing, for a boy from a poor background with a pretty rotten job, the army would have been an appealing prospect in many ways. It was a career, a steady job, soldiers were well fed and the money wasn't too bad: a private earned a shilling a day, with an additional penny for every day spent in a war zone (raised to 3d a day in 1918), a little better than George Fortune's 3/6 a week for those long hours at the barber's shop and Fred Dixon's 5 shillings a week as a stationer's runner.

At the same time, however, Edward would have had some idea of the horrors taking place on the fields of France and Flanders. His uncle had been killed. Many of his contemporaries from Admiral Place had gone to war; a few of them were never coming home. At this distance it's impossible to know what Edward's motivations or reservations would have been but, whether he was called up or volunteered, he entered the army at the age of eighteen, and I strongly suspect that he was first sent over to Flanders in the spring of 1918 once the law regarding nineteen-year-olds was relaxed. The 10th Queen's had suffered heavy casualties in the German Spring Offensive and they needed to make up the numbers fast. One account of the 10th Queen's mentions the arrival of 'a load of nineteen-year-olds' as new recruits around that time, and when the National Archives made the wills of soldiers available in 2012 I found Edward's, made on 2 April 1918, three weeks short of his nineteenth birthday.

If the accounts above are anything to go by, there was no sense of fear among the young lads at enlistment. There was just a feeling that it was something you had to do, something that got you out of the routine of industrial life, something that promised adventure and something that made you feel that you were genuinely contributing to the war effort.

Enlisting was only the start, however. The next step was to turn these youngsters into soldiers. Meanwhile, I was trying to turn myself into a walker.

6

'I AM THE KING OF ENGLAND TODAY, BUT HEAVEN KNOWS WHAT I MAY BE TOMORROW'

I left what had been Gadsden Mews, re-emerged from the shadow of Trellick Tower into the glorious spring sunshine, made for central London, passed through Hyde Park and Victoria, walked through Westminster, over the river and onto the Thames Path. As I reached Bermondsey, the sky bruised and darkened, a chill wind blew up and the heavens opened. There wasn't another soul on the Thames Path, and I walked for two and a half hours through Bermondsey, Rotherhithe and Deptford with the relentless *pock, pock* of raindrops on my waterproof and millions of pinpricks bursting on the grey-brown surface of the river. I was glad that I could stay at home that first night.

The next day my route through my native South-East London into Kent was arrow-straight and I was able to walk all the way out past the M25 without need for deviation until I reached Dartford, one of the first towns in the country to take in significant numbers of refugees fleeing the fighting on the Western Front. Within weeks of war being declared, bewildered Belgians began arriving in Dartford to

be at first installed in the less-than-salubrious surroundings
of the local workhouse before most were settled with oblig-
ing local families. Many found jobs in the town, including
at the local Vickers munitions factory, where they made
shells that could feasibly have ended up landing in their own
back yard.

Such was the Belgian presence in Dartford that at one
point a Belgian café opened, and the town began to take on
a distinctly cosmopolitan air. The German prisoners of war
in local hospitals before they were transferred to camps, as
well as the arrival of Australian and American wounded,
meant that the walls of the wards echoed with a range of
accents and languages and, given the pain most of these
men were in, rarely can so many swear words in so many
languages and dialects have been heard in one place.

Further east I arrived one sunny spring afternoon in
Gravesend, which was the scene of one of the war's more
curious incidents. Captain Robert Campbell of the 1st
Battalion, East Surrey Regiment, had been a reservist before
the war and was among the first to cross the Channel with
the British Expeditionary Force in July 1914. A month later
he was badly wounded near Mons – possibly he was one of
the men left behind that troubled Walter Cook's uncle
Robert so much and led to Walter's enlistment – captured
and taken to a military hospital in Cologne, from where he
was transferred to a prisoner-of-war camp in Magdeburg.

Two years into his internment, Campbell learned that his
mother was gravely ill back home in Gravesend. Helpless
and frustrated behind the wire of a prison camp far from
home, and with nothing to lose, he wrote a letter to the

Kaiser asking to be granted permission to see his mother one last time. Campbell must have been surprised to receive a reply at all, let alone one in which the German monarch granted him two weeks' leave from the camp, relying on his honour as an officer to ensure his return within the time allowed.

Campbell made his way back to Kent by train and boat via the Netherlands, arriving home on 7 November to spend a week in Gravesend with his ailing parent. Captain Campbell was sure to depart again in good time to honour the terms of the Kaiser's dispensation and returned to Germany to see out the remainder of the war in the Magdeburg camp. Mrs Campbell died eight weeks later.

Leaving Gravesend I rejoined Watling Street at Strood, walked along the western bank of the Medway, turned left over the bridge and crossed to Rochester, its castle high on a promontory before me as the ancient town woke up, stretched and prepared to embark on a warm spring Saturday. Skirting the centre, I turned along the riverside esplanade and followed the Medway south. On the outskirts of Rochester I was at last able to leave the sole-bruising hardness of tarmac and paving stone to join the waymarked North Downs Way, the national trail that would escort me the remaining fifty-odd miles to Dover and the English Channel. It was a steady climb onto the Downs, passing the churned chalky grey of recently ploughed fields, until in a break in the trees that lined the path I spied Kit's Coty, a trio of ancient standing stones topped by a large, heavy capstone just off the path at the edge of a field.

This is purportedly the location of a great battle that took place in the middle of the fifth century, at which Vortigern and his forces took on the Jute army of Hengist and Horsa, whose assistance he had solicited for his own domestic power struggles only for the Jutes to decide they quite fancied sticking around and running the place themselves. The 'Kit' of the name is thought to come from Catigern, a son of Vortigern, who died on the battlefield that day and whose grave the 'coty' is purported to be. It is definitely an ancient grave of some kind: a barrow some seventy feet in length used to be visible until centuries of ploughing levelled the ground, leaving this clutch of ancient stones encased by railings at the edge of the field as the only apparent remnant of a battle that no one is actually certain even took place. Its mysterious provenance has made the Coty an attraction for visitors for centuries: George Orwell passed by in the 1930s, while Samuel Pepys pronounced it 'a thing of great antiquity and I am mightily glad to see it'.

It's an incongruous sight, this *pi* symbol in three dimensions: a grave from a possibly mythical fight in a farmer's field high on the North Downs. There's even some doubt that Vortigern and his sons even existed, making this visit to Kit's Coty practically the antithesis of my own quest. Here was an event and people whose lives and stories might possibly have been conjured from thin air, or loosely based on facts, that had lasted through many centuries, while I was making a journey to find someone who had certainly existed, yet had passed entirely from memory within a generation of his death.

In the afternoon I rested for a while on a bench at the top of the village of Detling, next to its RAF memorial, before pressing on, passing through some of Kent's – and England's – most beautiful countryside. I had found a good walking rhythm at this stage and my steps and breathing were in perfect tandem, creating an almost trance-like state in which I rarely looked up from a spot on the road a few yards in front of me. The miles and hours were disappearing under my feet on a flat, single-track road, as I headed east between rape fields of deep-green stalks sprinkled lightly with yellow that would be ablaze with colour a week or two hence.

After what must have been a good hour or more after leaving Detling, I lifted my gaze from the tarmac in front of me and was stopped dead in my tracks. I'm not usually one for postcard representations of England. For me, a suburban street of terraced houses with a Mace on the corner evokes England as much as an ivy-clad thatched cottage with a well in the garden, but the sight that greeted me there on the road somewhere in Kent was enough to terminate my walking rhythm and bring me to a toe-crunching halt.

The day was easing towards late afternoon and the fledgling shadows were just gaining the confidence to commence lengthening. In the field to my right two horses, one brown, one white, grazed lazily, the late afternoon sun warming every detail and contour of their bodies. Behind them, the white-tipped conical roofs of two oast houses peeped over some trees, while in the distance a square church tower interrupted the hazy horizon. Above the idyllic scene was a bright-blue canopy marked only with a few cotton-wool puffs of cloud. Somewhere up there, a skylark was singing its tiny lungs out as, in the distance, the church bell began to ring.

This was just the kind of idyll for which the soldiers were told they were fighting: the classic image of England, the type of scene crying out for a soundtrack by Vaughan Williams and captured by generations of painters. It was a vista that had remained unchanged for a good couple of centuries, the same bell tolling for generations, the same birdsong from the heavens, the same shadows stretching across the grass year after year. I stood for a while, watching nothing in particular yet watching everything: history, nature and society in a view utterly devoid of people but which has somehow come to define a people.

Once I'd got moving again, perhaps lulled too far by this watercolour perfection and having spied on the map a dotted green line that represented a more direct public footpath route to Harrietsham, I left the waymarked security of the North Downs Way to struggle clumsily across a recently ploughed field. Too accustomed to the well-trodden, signposted trail, I'd been tempted into a shortcut, one I messed up and led to me straying unawares into a wood that turned out to be private property. Ahead of me I heard the throaty rumble of a quad bike on which a man dressed in a green sweatshirt and combat trousers appeared, pulled up, switched off the engine and regarded me as if he'd just walked into his living room and found me sitting in his favourite armchair flicking through the television channels. Fortunately his initial save-it-for-the-judge-bucko demeanour as I explained where I thought I was soon gave way to a helpful point in the direction of the public footpath I'd believed I was on. Thankfully he'd realised he was just dealing with an incompetent buffoon with barely cursory map-reading skills rather than someone intent on pilfering birds' eggs or putting on some kind of free festival. He even gave me a cheery 'happy hiking' as he gunned the quad bike and plunged back into the undergrowth.

Once on the right path – which turned out to be ankle-deep in mud – I arrived in Harrietsham just as the shadows disappeared into the twilight and lights were winking on behind thick cottage walls. The weatherboarded Roebuck Inn was blue-white in the gloom, and I stayed there the night, my feet sore and my face tingling from the unseasonably warm weather. Warm though it was – strangely so for late March – even in the height of summer the fate of the long-distance walker is such that one is forced to crank up the radiators to ensure the underwear and socks rinsed out in the sink are dry by the morning.

It was another sunny day as I headed out of the village the next morning to pick up the trail. After half a mile or so I came upon a bench, at one end of which sat a full-sized wooden sculpture of a fat friar cheerfully asleep, with his head resting in his hand to remind you that this path was also part of the ancient Pilgrim's Way. I sat with him for a while, looking out across the valley as the Sunday morning church bells echoed around the villages, and could easily have joined him in a morning snooze if I hadn't needed to be in Wye by sunset.

Late in the afternoon I stopped to rest at a ruined church by a lake below a grand old house. All that remained were a tower, a small section of wall and a tiny side chapel. St Mary's, Eastwell, dates back to the fifteenth century, and the flint-built tower in front of me was part of this original construction. It was a peaceful, shady spot and I ended up staying longer than I'd anticipated, poking around the graveyard, reading the stones and just sitting looking through the trees to the lake and listening to the birdsong echoing from inside a belfry long ago relieved of its bells.

I was sitting on a stone slab that, judging by the remains of the walls around me, was once inside the main body of the church. St Mary's had been badly damaged during the Second World War, then all but abandoned afterwards. In earlier times it would have been the place of worship for the family and workers of the Eastwell Place estate, but presumably an evolving social structure and the impact of the Second World War had seen the congregation decline almost to nothing. When the roof fell in in 1951 repair seemed pointless. The nave and everything but the tower, the small stretch of wall and the little chapel were demolished and removed in 1956, leaving just a tranquil ruin to be gently reclaimed by nature.

I didn't realise until I stood up to leave, but the slab on which I'd been resting my weary bottom was actually the key to the greatest story associated with St Mary's. It's a rectangular rubble-brick construction with a flat stone top, on the front of which is a plaque that's quite hard to decipher unless you squat down in front of it and look closely, to read: 'Reputed to be the tomb of Richard Plantagenet, 22 December 1550'.

Richard Plantagenet, who was born around 1470, was an illegitimate son of Richard III, a boy raised in isolation, living and working with a tutor with very occasional visits from a man dressed in fine clothes the only break in the routine of endless one-to-one study. One day in 1485 the teenage Richard was hurriedly dressed by the tutor, put onto a horse and taken on a long journey that ended at a field in Leicestershire full of tents and apprehensive-looking soldiers: this was the eve of the Battle of Bosworth Field, the ultimate showdown of the Wars of the Roses. Young Richard was shown into the grandest tent of them all, where someone he recognised as the man who had been visiting him for as long as he could remember introduced himself as his father. If that wasn't surprise enough for someone who had met few people other than the old boy who drummed Latin declensions into him, the man in the tent continued, 'My boy, I am the King of England today, but heaven knows what I may be tomorrow, for the rebels are strong. If the Earl of Richmond wins the day he will seek out Plantagenets wherever they may be and crush them. Tell no one, absolutely no one, who you are unless I am victorious.' This was to be Richard's last meeting and only conversation with his father.

The following day's battle brought a bloody end to the reign of the Plantagenets in England, and when news filtered back from the fight that his father had been killed, the younger Richard immediately made himself scarce. He fled to London and commenced an apprenticeship as a stonemason, a trade he would continue for the rest of his life.

In 1540 Sir Thomas Moyle employed an elderly mason in the building of his home and estate at Eastwell Place, a man who would stay working on the project for a full ten years until his death. Moyle noticed that the older man stayed aloof from the rest of the builders and masons, and he became, from a distance, fascinated by this enigmatic, faintly melancholy old workman. It was some time in the mid-1540s, when Moyle noticed the mason reading a text in Latin – most unusual for a labouring man – that he engaged him in conversation and eventually coaxed Richard's story out of him. On hearing of Richard's royal connections Moyle allowed this last of the Plantagenets to build himself a small cottage on the estate in which to live out his final years. He was buried on the estate and the tomb where I'd parked my rear end is his reputed last resting place.

It's a terrific story and one that I find myself hoping to be true. But as I looked at the tomb in what would have once been the nave of the church, I was well aware that wishing something to be true doesn't make it so. I thought about Richard and I thought about Catigern of Kit's Coty, both victims in different ways of wars and battles, and both possibly nothing like the men of their respective legends. These mythologies made me think about Edward: in a way I was mythologising him by trying to recreate his story and fashion his personality. Through the character traits and personal attributes I was attaching to him every time I imagined his experiences, I was creating a myth. The sketchy account of the basic movements of his regiment in the 10th Queen's Royal West Surreys' war diary provided the only clues I had to where he was and what he was doing in his final months, and even that was vague. I had no idea where Edward had been or what he was doing, and certainly I had no idea about who he actually was. Most disappointingly of all, I had no idea how, where or why he died. Was he single-handedly charging a machine-gun post and saving countless lives in exchange for his own? Was he taken out by an artillery shell while advancing across no man's land? Did he absent-mindedly stick his head above the trench parapet just as a sniper fixed him in his sights? Was his death heroic, tragic or even comic? At the back of my mind I was even starting to wonder whether the decades of silence that followed his end had something to do with the nature of his death. Could he, I wondered, even have been one of the 300 or so British soldiers court-martialled and shot by their own side? Hero, traitor, coward or deserter, I reminded myself that I might never know for certain the truth behind Edward's final days and death. Despite this resignation I still had to be careful not to create a mythology that might be at best misleading and at worst a gross distortion of the truth, even though I might never learn what the truth actually was.

I heaved my rucksack onto my back and set off again, passing Sir Thomas Moyle's old Eastwell Manor, now inevitably a hotel and conference centre, and walked up the hill towards the village green of Boughton Aluph.

7

'IN THE EVENT OF
MY DEATH ...'

Basic training for new recruits took place in Britain, either at an established camp like Aldershot or Shorncliffe, near Folkestone, or one of the many new camps that sprang up as the war progressed. Initially, the emphasis was on getting the recruits fit, teaching them about their equipment and how to use it, and instilling discipline. For most of the new lads this was a completely alien way of life: the endless drills, the constant cleaning and polishing of equipment, how to salute a superior officer correctly, how to dig a trench and the route marches of up to twenty-five miles with a fully equipped pack. They were given a number, a haircut and a uniform, as the army set about stripping them of as much of their individuality as it took to make them into fighting and killing machines.

On arrival there was another, more rigorous medical for which the men had to strip naked and wait in line to see the doctor, who would prod every limb, check the pulse, examine the teeth and test eyesight and hearing.

The new recruit was then given his basic kit: two tunics, two pairs of trousers, an overcoat, a cap, a pair of boots, three pairs of socks, two pairs of underwear, three shirts, a set of cutlery, a mess tin, a razor, toothbrush, shaving brush, shoe brush and a needle and cotton. With the kit the quartermaster handed the new man some string and brown paper: civilian clothes, the last link to a previous life, were to be wrapped up and sent home.

One of the positive aspects of camp life was the three meals a day, something men from poorer backgrounds would not have been used to. Breakfast consisted of bacon with kippers or a slice of bread and a mug of tea. Lunch was pie, stew or boiled beef and potatoes, while at tea time you were provided with bread and jam and more tea. The helpings were not enormous, and with all the relentless physical exercise the younger recruits were often hungry, meaning they were thankful for the recreation huts set up by churches and voluntary organisations where the lads could go to sit in the evening with a cup of tea and a bun.

George Fortune was sent initially to Hounslow Barracks with the Royal Fusiliers but then moved on to Aldershot with the Middlesex Regiment, where he was soon given a taste of what military life had in store.

'When we arrived at Aldershot we had to parade at the gym for a lecture from the adjutant,' said George. 'He was a little man, I think he was Jewish, name was Lewis. He jumped up on the platform and shouted, "I'll break your hearts!" Someone wrote to *John Bull* about him and in the article he was referred to as the Khaki Heartbreaker.'

In order to build up fitness, George and his colleagues were marched constantly around the square in all weathers in a training regime that bordered on the brutal: 'They would have us up at five in the morning, shaking blankets out on the square, then for the rest of the day they drilled the life out of us. Our hands used to be at our sides. The weather was freezing and I got bad chilblains: my hands were like sausages and the chilblains were broken too. Waiting for pay outside our barracks one day Sergeant Watts – he was a real snaggle-toothed bastard – came up to me, barked, "Take your hands out of your pockets," and slashed at them with his cane. I was a bit slow getting them out as they were so sore. When I hadn't whipped them out as quickly as he'd liked, he asked me my name and told me to fall in once I'd got my pay. When I went to see him he made me clean metal washbasins with sand. The water was ice cold and the sand got into my broken chilblains, and since 1919 I've been looking for that bastard. It's not too late to kill him.'

William Dann's experience of his basic training was altogether less unpleasant. After enlisting, he was billeted at home for six weeks and drilled at Preston Park in Brighton before being sent to Canterbury where he was transferred to the 10th Queen's as an infantryman.

'The training I thoroughly enjoyed,' he said. 'It was so exciting with plenty of interesting things to do. The discipline was a bit tight, but you could take it – that's what you went in for. After a while at Canterbury we were transferred to Colchester Barracks, which was an infantry barracks. The officer shouted at parade one morning, "All men under nineteen remain and the rest dismiss." They gave us all a form and a railway warrant home to get our parents' permission to go to France, even though we were still under nineteen. I went back to Brighton and my father and I had a chat. He asked me if I wanted to go and I said, "Well, I've been with these chaps a long time and I know them. If I don't go I'll have to make new friends, so I think I'd rather go.'"

William Dann was going to France. Meanwhile Fred Dixon also found himself training at Canterbury, working with horses: 'We had the stiffest training with the 6th Dragoon Guards at Canterbury. It was the dragoon depot down there and we came under the instruction of the peacetime sergeants, who were a tough lot. They tried to impress upon us what a subhuman breed we were; if they set out to break our hearts they didn't succeed, but it wasn't for want of trying.'

The recruits were roused at 5:30 a.m. by a bugler playing 'Reveille'. Not only was this to wake the men, it also told them that they were required on parade fifteen minutes later washed, shaved and clad in shorts, singlets and plimsolls. After parade they'd be given breakfast and sent on a four-mile run, at the end of which they were required to clear a succession of horse jumps. Finally they were sent into the stables.

'That's when Sergeant Jock Simpson entered the arena, bade us good morning in an appropriate fashion – "Now then you bloody shower of bastards" – and had us commence the mucking out,' said Fred. 'This consisted of removing the horses' bedding with our hands and taking it outside to dry off and use again. The sergeants were very particular about us removing every piece of straw. Then grooming and feeding followed, then the cookhouse rang – no time to wash our hands – then we dressed for parade, then the real ordeal of the day, a terror: one hour in the riding school, much of the time without stirrups. At the end of the hour we'd emerge from the school sweating, with grimy faces, dusty uniforms, and the horses were all white foam.'

In Bradford, Horace Calvert was also commencing his basic training. At first he was billeted at home, reporting to Belle Vue Barracks every morning to parade and drill from 9:30 until lunchtime. After a week he was given a uniform, and a week after that their rifles arrived.

'We got a khaki jacket, then trousers, socks, puttees, heavy marching boots, cap, badge, brass numerals for our shoulder straps and a greatcoat, but no other kit because we were still living at home,' he recalled. 'Puttees came with practice, till you knew exactly how many turns there were on each leg. They were awkward, but they supported you. Much better than thick stockings in that respect.'

As a change from the parade ground, twice a week Horace and the other recruits would be marched through the town as a recruiting exercise. Men intending to join up were encouraged to fall in behind the unit and follow them back to the barracks to begin the process.

'Sometimes there'd be twenty or thirty behind you,' he said. 'Some lined up because of drink, I'm sure. We definitely seemed to bring in a few when the pubs had shut in the afternoon. The crowds all clapped and cheered: I enjoyed it and I was proud. The other recruits were very friendly and you'd all help one another.'

Being an underage recruit did have its drawbacks, however: 'At that time King George V had made it known that he liked all members of his household brigade to have a moustache, so the chaps all grew one – but I couldn't. I was only sixteen and hadn't started to shave yet. I tried to start shaving, and using a razor, but nothing was happening. I even got extra fatigues, peeling potatoes and what have you, for not growing a moustache, but I took it all in good part.'

Victor Fagence, a farmer's son from Surrey, had volunteered almost reluctantly for the 10th Queen's in December 1915, a few weeks before the first conscription bill was passed. He was eighteen years old.

'There were pressures on me, such as how all the young men around my age had joined up, but I was rather fed up with things in general,' he remembered. 'Eventually, I thought, Well, I'll have to go in the army before long anyway so I might as well join up rather than wait for the Conscription Act. I was posted to the 10th Queen's at Battersea, given six days' leave before I had to report and then reported a few days before Christmas at the battalion headquarters at Lavender Hill. I gave them my papers and was measured up for my uniform. By the time I joined, the war had been on about sixteen months and the uniform suppliers were better than they had been in the early days. It wasn't made to measure but I was fitted out pretty well.'

The 10th Queen's would train in Battersea Park with a similar intention to Horace Calvert's marches through Bradford: to encourage others to enlist. They'd have squad drills, bayonet practice with straw-filled sacks, and marching in column, but the effect seemed to Victor to be negligible: 'People would watch us train in Battersea Park but by then everybody was used to seeing troops and soldiers everywhere so we were nothing special.'

In January 1916 the battalion moved on to Aldershot, where they learned skills that would come in useful but couldn't really be indulged in Battersea Park: trench digging, sandbag filling and the laying of barbed wire. It would be a while, though, before Victor could use those skills in earnest.

'The government had given a pledge that no man under the age of nineteen would see active service,' he said. 'But I think with me it was discovered by accident that I'd put a year on my age when I joined. So, when the 10th went to France in May 1916, I was sent to the 12th Battalion in Northampton, a reserve battalion.'

Alan Short from Bromley-by-Bow in East London was born a month after Edward, in May 1899, the son of a lighterman on the River Thames. He left school in 1914 and worked at the Joseph Rank flour company, in Leadenhall Street in the City of London, and had experienced the reality of the war when the first boy from his local church had been killed in May 1915.

'Alfred Ernest Crawthorne. He was older than me but he was a friend of the family,' said Alan. 'He'd helped carry me around the playground to celebrate my elevation to the main school from junior school. He was a very nice man. I knew his two brothers and they took it hard. The families were more or less left to fend for themselves. One conveyed one's sympathy but there was no spare money in the community to support them.'

After losing his job in a dispute over wages in January 1917, Alan decided to join up, despite still being four months short of his eighteenth birthday: 'I went to Stratford in East London. I didn't want to be called a conscript; it indicated that you weren't too keen on going. I knew that I was approaching military age, when I could be called up, so I just went myself. I sat there, was called forward, signed forms to join the service for the duration of the war, took the oath of allegiance and got a shilling, which I immediately went out and spent on riotous living.'

Alan was called up to the Training Reserve, a battalion of underage boys that were given a year's training in England before they could go out to the Front. With his friend Ernest Moyes he reported to Horse Guards Parade, where they joined around fifty other boys and marched to Paddington Station. From there, they were taken by train to Sutton Veny Camp, near Warminster.

'The others came mostly from East London too, and some of them were already pretty tough,' he said. 'There were huts for about thirty men at a time. Your bed was a low trestle, three planks, a short mattress and pillow, and a couple of blankets. After "Reveille" they were packed up and your mattress had to be folded over, all very regimental. The inspections were pretty thorough – they even insisted you had no mud between the studs on your shoes.'

Like most of the youngsters hoping for a bit of adventure, Alan found the monotony and routine of camp life took a little getting used to: 'The day would start at 6, and if you were struggling to get up the sergeant would tip your bed up and out you'd get. Then you folded up your mattress and dry-scrubbed your floor with a short-haired brush. Breakfast was mostly bread and butter and tea. I don't remember any bacon and eggs … Then there'd be training till lunch, and my favourite was a lovely meat pie with a soft thick crust:

the quality was good. Then there'd be more training. I found the constant drilling a bit boring, but it meant you learned to stand to attention and obey commands. We learned how to throw bombs too – you got the bomb, pulled the pin out and threw it round arm. I could manage about thirty feet. The bombs were about the size of your hand and were quite comfortable. There were a lot of accidents but I was never nervous with it. Some of the fellas were, but if you followed instructions you were perfectly safe. If a man did a thing wrong they'd call him this, that and the other. It upset me in the beginning but you got hardened to it.'

Basic training was usually completed in around six weeks and, depending on the state of the war and how urgently recruits were needed at the Front, full training could last anything up to five months.

Eventually, the new recruits would receive word that they were to be sent over to France, at which point they would be issued with their combat kit: a steel helmet, body belt, field dressings, gas mask and ground sheet, goggles and vests.

It was around this time that the soldiers would make their wills. If the nerves and the cold, creeping fear of impending departure hadn't done it, and if the last vestiges of glamour, flag-waving crowds and cheers had not been battered out of the men by the relentless drilling, being handed a folded piece of paper marked 'Informal Will' and told to complete it would have been the final realisation that this was actually happening. They were going to war and there was a strong chance they wouldn't be coming back.

When the British Probate Office made thousands of soldiers' wills available online in 2013 I managed to find a scan of Edward's, one of the saddest documents I've ever seen. It's in his handwriting, controlled and well-practised, if slightly spidery, and it's dated 2 April 1918, seven months almost to the day before his death. There isn't much space on the single sheet, and the writing bunches up a little towards the bottom of the page where he's signed and dated it, with his rank and regiment, but it's clear and coherent:

In the event of my death, I leave my War Savings Certificates to my goddaughter, Miss Lily S Hill of No. 6 Spencer Street, Southall, and £2 to my grandmother Mrs Christopher, No. 5 Branstone Street, N Kensington, the remainder of my money and effects going to my mother, Mrs G. Connelly, No 6 Branstone Street, N Kensington.

And that's it. That's all Edward Connelly seems to have left behind of himself: fewer than fifty words of right-sloping handwriting, conventional in its well-practised flourishes and loops, and clearly carefully thought out. I wonder where he was when he wrote it. Surrounded by similar lads to him, the George Fortunes, Fred Dixons and Horace Calverts, sitting on their beds hunched over these flimsy pieces of paper following the guidelines they'd been given as to what to write?

'In the event of my death ...' What a thing for an eighteen-year-old to have to write, miles from home in a strange place, in an unreal world of drills and orders and bugle calls and bomb-throwing practice. How he must have longed to be at home among those familiar cramped streets, still just yards from where he was born, and see his mother and father and grandparents again. Instead he had to prepare to sail for a foreign country, departing Britain for the first time a matter of weeks after leaving Kensal Town for the first time.

As he thought about the event of his death, he thought about his goddaughter, his grandmother and his mother, arguably the three people closest to him in the world. He didn't have much to leave, a couple of quid, some savings certificates and the odd few coins and bits and pieces, but he shared them out thoughtfully. That was his legacy, all he had in the world.

(Lily S. Hill, incidentally, wasn't dealt much of a better hand by fate than her godfather. Barely a year old when Edward was making her the first beneficiary of his will, Lily married in March 1937 but within six months was dead from a lung abscess.)

The image of all those young lads, lined up in regimented rows, sitting on their bunks, hundreds of them, all just setting out in life, not even having got to grips with the world yet, not even having discovered who they are, is a powerful one; all of them hunched over like khaki-clad beetles, concentrating, making sure they used their best handwriting as they formed the words, 'In the event of my death …'

8

'IF YOU ARE NOT IN KHAKI BY THE 20TH, I SHALL CUT YOU DEAD'

The stone cross of the Boughton Aluph war memorial stood silhouetted starkly against the sky, with around thirty names from the First World War, including three sets of brothers.

I couldn't really define why but there was something particularly forbidding about this memorial. It could have been that the sun had gone in, the wind was whipping up and the late afternoon was turning chilly. Boughton Aluph has a large, triangular green, with houses and a pub on two sides embracing the village cricket field. The memorial stands away, on the furthest part of the green, facing away from the houses, with its back to the pub and cricket pitch. The image of its simple cross, stark against the grey sky as I'd approached, stuck with me, and later I investigated some of the names on the stone. They ranged from the teenaged to the middle-aged, and their deaths covered every year of the war (one man had even died in 1920, the result of injuries and shock sustained by being wounded and buried alive in a shell explosion).

There are thousands of these memorials in Britain (estimates of their numbers range wildly between 54,000 and 70,000), each of them the gateway to stories and lives, some remembered, some forgotten. Every one of those thousands of memorials can be taken individually, and a narrative of the Great War constructed from them – from vast, ornate, mournful angel-topped plaques listing hundreds of dead in the centre of a city to a handful of names on a simple stone in a remote hamlet, the story of one is the story of them all. The story I was pursuing is multiplied millions of times over by every man that went to war and never came back, every name on every last weather-beaten, forsaken, moss-smeared tablet that commemorates the fallen.

Continuing east I crossed the Great Stour, paused at the level crossing and arrived in Wye, grateful for a bed and a warm eyrie room high up in the King's Head. The window afforded a view across the rooftops to the giant crown carved into the hillside chalk to celebrate the coronation of Edward VII in 1902, as the nation came to terms with the end of the Victorian age and ushered in the Edwardian.

Early the following morning I found myself standing above the crown looking back at Wye from the opposite aspect. I continued over the top of the Downs through the villages of Stowting and Etchinghill, before arriving in Folkestone.

There was a chill in the streets as the sun slipped down behind the buildings, and after checking in at the hotel I headed into the town to find somewhere to eat. I walked into a restaurant where the only other occupants were a family group of about a dozen people, all of whom stopped talking and looked at me as I entered. The place was run by an earnest, suited man in his thirties who had the air of someone whose ambition had been something more than a small back-street establishment on the south coast. He was attentive and his manner was very proper, but there was a tired sadness about him. The suit didn't quite hang right, while his expression and complexion betrayed late nights and long melancholy days spent looking outside to a betting shop and a pawnbrokers, rather than a piazza or an azure sea.

The party at the next table stood up to leave in a flurry of hugs, good wishes and exhortations to 'come back safe' to a young man with dark hair and red cheeks. A woman turned away to roll a tissue under her lower eyelids, then switched on a beaming smile and turned to hug the young man long and hard. For most port towns the wrench of departure is a way of life, and that night it certainly appeared to be a feature of Folkestone. Wherever that young man was going, wherever he is now, he and everyone around that table would remember that night for a long time: the forced banter, the anecdotes, the nervous laughter, the awkward silences and in every mind the sound of the clock ticking down to inevitable departure.

Folkestone saw more than its fair share of departures during the First World War. Somewhere north of ten million people passed through Folkestone between 1914 and 1918, mostly soldiers but also some 800,000 Red Cross and nursing staff, and around 3,500 German prisoners of war. Countless others came back temporarily on leave, or for hospital treatment and convalescence. Walking back to my hotel through the deserted Monday-night streets where crisp packets and coffee cups were pushed around lazily by the breeze, it was hard to imagine this place as a key node in the winning of the war. When we think of the famous places of the First

World War it's fair to say that Folkestone lags considerably behind Ypres and Gallipoli, but it would be very wrong to underestimate the role it played throughout the conflict and the impact the war had on the town.

Folkestone found itself involved almost immediately war was declared, and in an unexpected way. 'Within a few days,' wrote J.C. Carlile in an account of Folkestone's war, published within months of the armistice, '285 German reservists arrived at the harbour to join the Kaiser's forces. They were detained on the grounds that the time allowed for enemy aliens to leave the country had expired. They did not seem distressed by the news.'

Life in the town kept up a veneer of normality, but being so physically close to the fighting it was inevitable that the odd nervous glance found its way towards the horizon. For one thing, when the wind was in the right direction the guns of the Western Front could be heard along much of the south coast.

'The air was thick with alarms,' wrote Carlile. 'There was a vague dread of something terrible – nobody was quite sure what. The coming of war cleared the roads of the pleasure cars that used to run by the river and through the lovely countryside to Canterbury, the cradle of English history. The sportsmen no longer followed the hounds, they went to face the Huns. The days became serious. Men looked over the seas with a touch of apprehension and before the end of the year the light of the moon was no longer a delight. The little comedy of life was blotted out by the tragedy of war.'

While most of the traffic through Folkestone was heading further south, there was some movement the other way.

When in August the first Belgian refugees arrived in the town in a pathetic flotilla of fishing boats and coal barges, the reality of the conflict was immediately brought home to the people of Folkestone. So traumatised were the Belgians that some even refused to leave the boats when they arrived, staring glassy-eyed and terrified at the locals gathered on the quayside to receive them.

Carlile described a heartrending scene: 'Each boat brought a cargo of humanity like dumb-driven cattle. Their plight was pitiful. Some had been in the train for a day and a night, others on the road for several days, but with little food. Few had any clothing, except the garments they were wearing. One white-haired old dame came in carpet slippers, not having been able to secure her boots in the hurry and panic to escape the Hun. Their presence was our first glimpse of the terrible reality of war.'

This reality manifested itself in other ways. The quality and availability of food was greatly reduced in the once-prosperous town, and the well-to-do locals had to adjust both their expectations and their terminology.

'What we had looked upon as butter, margarine and lard now became "fats",' Carlile recalled, 'and certain delicacies with which, in the past, we had endeavoured to stimulate our jaded appetites were now known under the generic and hideously offensive title of "offal". Dear, respectable ladies held up their hands in pious horror when told they could have offal, and, forsooth, it was not nice to refined ears; but, *mirabile dictu*, it grew to be a cherished word. If you went to a tea party you were expected to take your own sugar. In fact, your first gay words on entering a house were, "I've brought my sugar," at the same time producing a dainty little silken bag, or, if you were rich and well-favoured, a costly but convenient silver pocket casket.'

For those less able to transport their sugar in silver pocket caskets, the changes in the licencing laws were felt more keenly than any effect on afternoon tea.

'The cry was for national efficiency and the maximum output of labour, not to mention the safeguarding of the troops from temptation,' Carlile recalled. 'Thus it became impossible to purchase drink save between the hours of 12 and 2:30 and between 6 and 8, and no officer or soldier proceeding overseas could, under any pretext whatever, be served. This led to not a little indignation, and, indeed, it did seem to the superficial mind something more than a hardship that those who were on their way to the sternest possible duty – to face the hideous perils of modern warfare – were denied their glass, while those living at home in comfort and relative safety could have what they liked to pay for.'

Folkestone also has the dubious distinction of being the birthplace of the Order of the White Feather. It was started by the septuagenarian Admiral Charles Penrose-Fitzgerald, for whom age was not diminishing the fiery patriotism that had fuelled a long and distinguished naval career. Indeed, as early as 1904 Penrose-Fitzgerald was telling everyone who would listen that a war with Germany was required in order to maintain Britain's naval supremacy (something of which the Germans took note and ensured the German navy was strengthened accordingly in the coming years).

When war finally arrived a full decade later than he'd have liked, the feisty admiral was appalled on his perambulations around town to see young men still promenading around Folkestone wearing baggy slacks and swinging tennis rackets while all around them a blur of khaki passed by on their way to the harbour, to France and the good fight. Glaring at them through his monocle, whiskers a-twitch, Admiral Penrose-Fitzgerald resolved to do something about these braying, shirking gawd-help-uses. In the late summer of 1914 he somehow persuaded around thirty young women to lurk on the seafront, accost any young man of military age not in uniform and present him with a white feather as a symbol of cowardice. The idea was to shame the men into enlisting, and there's no doubt that a few men did subsequently slink off guiltily to enlist.

However, while there undoubtedly were men who were reluctant to join up until they really had to, the indiscriminate nature of the feather campaign meant that it was as likely to target a man who'd tried to enlist but been turned down, or who was engaged in war work at home, as someone who might be a war-dodger. There were numerous cases of women pressing white feathers into the hands of men who were home from the front on leave or had even been sent home wounded (one soldier, on leave, out of uniform and accosted on a tram by a feather-wafting woman, came up with the splendid response, 'I'm in civvies because people think my uniform might be lousy, but if I had it on I wouldn't be half as lousy as you'). Perhaps the most ill-advised white feather was the one presented to George Samson on a bus in Carnoustie in 1915. Samson was wearing civilian clothes and travelling on the bus because he was on his way to a reception to honour his award of the Victoria Cross, given for gallantry at Gallipoli, where he had also been seriously wounded.

In the decades that followed the war it appeared the shaming was turned on its head. When the BBC was preparing its landmark documentary series *The Great War* in the 1960s, it appealed for some of the 'white feather girls' to come forward: they received only two replies, one of whom confessed that in hindsight she felt like a 'proper chump'.

It wasn't just feathers, either: some women were so determined that their menfolk should enlist they went to great lengths to show it and warn of the potential consequences. In July 1915 this small advertisement appeared in *The Times*: 'Jack F.G.: If you are not in khaki by the 20th, I shall cut you dead. Ethel M' (apparently a Berlin newspaper correspondent got hold of this, misunderstood the vernacular and published it translated as, 'If you are not in khaki by the 20th, I shall hack you to death').

Aside from the distribution of feathers and the constant transit of troops between the town and the continent, the war truly came to Folkestone at the end of a Friday afternoon on 25 May 1917. A small group of German aircraft had been deterred from a bombing raid over London by low cloud. Determined not to have had an entirely wasted mission, they focused instead on Folkestone as they made their way back to base. Having dropped bombs on the Shorcliffe military camp just west of the town, the Gotha biplanes then flew over central Folkestone, its streets packed with late-afternoon shoppers and strollers ahead of what promised to be a gloriously sunny weekend.

There were sporadic air raids in England throughout the war. Nothing on the scale of the Blitz, of course, but when biplanes replaced the unwieldy zeppelins it became much easier to make short, quick and efficient raids on London and the south of England. The casualties were usually on a comparatively small scale – nearby Dover was bombed on eighteen separate occasions during the war, resulting in a total of twenty-two deaths – but that would change as the shadows lengthened over Folkestone that day and soldiers and civilians made their last shopping trips of the week, milling and dawdling beneath the awnings of Tontine Street.

It's still a busy shopping street today. Next to a gallery that used to be the Brewery Tap pub (and which retains the pub's rather beautiful tiled frontage advertising Mackeson's Hythe Ales) is a small paved area with a plaque commemorating what happened there shortly before 6 p.m. that Friday evening.

One bomb was all it took. Several fell on Folkestone that afternoon: some exploded harmlessly, others failed to go off (including one that crashed through a hotel from roof to basement). Another killed a valet outside Folkestone Central station trying to calm a pair of horses agitated by the bangs and chaos. But the bomb that fell onto the road outside the Stokes Brothers grocery shop in the middle of a packed Tontine Street killed a startling sixty-one people, mostly women, mostly children. Their ages ranged across the full three score years and ten: the eldest victim was 72-year-old widow Katherine Laxton; the youngest was two-month-old Walter Moss, killed along with his mother,

Annie, while his father, George, was away at the Front. Another young victim was two-year-old Dennis Hayes, who also died alongside his mother, who in turn had been widowed when her husband had been killed on the Somme a year earlier. It was a scene of utter carnage and devastation, unparalleled and unprecedented in Britain in its scale and the indiscriminate nature of the killing.

For me, though, perhaps the most affecting victim of the Folkestone air raid was killed not outside the Stokes Brothers shop, but a short distance away on Shorncliffe Road. Sixteen-year-old Doris Eileen Spencer Walton, the South African-born daughter of a wealthy businessman, was playing a game of tennis on a lawn at Athelstan School. Aware of the distant booms among the giggling and shrieking of the game, Doris would probably not have felt unduly threatened. The war was somewhere else for most people; when you were a sixteen-year-old girl enjoying a game of tennis ahead of a weekend of more games and cream teas it must have seemed almost non-existent. After all, the thuds of guns from the camp and the anti-aircraft batteries along the coast were familiar now, not to mention the occasional sound of artillery brought across the Channel on the breeze.

One of the bombs fell near enough to stop the game temporarily but far enough away for the girls not to be in danger. Alas, by sheer fluke, a fizzing fragment of hot, sharp metal arced into the tennis court and struck Doris in the head, killing her instantly.

I walked back to my hotel through the pedestrianised centre of Folkestone in the dark, finding it hard to match this deserted, monochrome town with the hive of activity and tragedy it had been a century earlier. I thought about Doris Walton and the noise, chaos and tragedy of Tontine Street, and I thought of the blur of khaki that had passed through this town for the duration of the war. I thought of the young man at the restaurant and how his story replicated an incalculable number of similar departures, the ones between 1914 and 1918 having particular poignancy. It was an unusually warm spring but a chill wind pulled at my clothes and blew specks of grit into my face. Light flooded onto the pavement from a convenience store as I passed, inside which the shopkeeper and a man were shouting and pointing at each other. I quickened my step and hurried back to the hotel. I walked parallel to the coast, glancing south at each junction towards the blackness of the sea, where France lay beyond the darkness and where the departures I'd been thinking about became arrivals.

9

'I WAS SEVENTEEN YEARS OLD AND ALREADY I WAS WELL ACQUAINTED WITH DEATH'

The first stage of the journey to the Front was the march to the local railway station. Early in the war there would often be a brass band at the head of the column; by the time of Edward's embarkation this ritual had largely been dispensed with. Most of the men crossed from Folkestone or Southampton and arrived at Boulogne or Le Havre, usually travelling overnight with an escort of destroyers in an attempt to make things difficult for German warships and U-boats. It would have been nothing like the crossing today: the troop ships would have been so crowded that men trying to sleep didn't even have enough room to stretch out. Night crossings would be in total darkness: men weren't even allowed to smoke for fear of the orange tip of a cigarette giving away their presence to the enemy. It was a long, slow crossing that would be unpleasant enough in calm waters, let alone a rough sea.

Once in France, the men would usually be taken to the massive training camp at Étaples, not far from Calais, an enormous facility capable of accommodating 100,000 men.

New recruits would be given more specific training pertinent to the battlefield – what to do in the event of a gas attack, how to dig trenches and build sandbag defences – and there would be more endless drilling and parades on the vast, sand-covered parade ground known throughout the Western Front as 'the bull ring'.

Horace Calvert's first crossing, in 1916, would have been typical: 'We were marched off with a band from the barracks at Chelsea with all our relatives behind, past Buckingham Palace and along Birdcage Walk to Waterloo station. Then we entrained for Southampton and were put on a troop ship that sailed after dark, escorted by British destroyers. On this troop ship they were selling tea and pies at inflated prices: they must have made a fortune with what they were charging. All your English money was dispensed with on board because it would be no good in France. The crew knew that and whacked the prices up accordingly. During the night I looked out and you could see the destroyers signalling to one another with lamps. We got into Le Havre just as dawn was breaking and were marched through the town and up to a camp a few miles from the town. There you were paraded and checked and ten or twelve of you sent to each tent.

'The next day you were taken to the training ground where they had trenches and you were given practice with throwing Mills bombs. I couldn't throw them very far so never became part of a bombing squad. You were also taught to dig trenches and fill sandbags: one held the bag open, the other filled it and when you got it into position you had a flat piece of wood and batted it into place. If they were well

packed and hard the better chance they had of stopping a
bullet.

'We had gas training, too, for which we were issued with
a flannelette thing with two eyepieces and a rubber tube
impregnated with some kind of chemical to neutralise the
gas. It was very hot and uncomfortable. Then the day came
when the draft were paraded and divided into battalions.
They started at one end: the biggest and tallest men were on
the flanks and these chaps were sent to the 1st Battalion. I
went to the 4th Battalion, Number 2 Company.'

George Fortune arrived in France with the 10th Queen's
a year later: 'Before we went on leave they cropped all our
hair. We looked like a lot of convicts. My mother came to
see me and swore I'd been in prison: she was only convinced
I hadn't when she saw me off on the train and I asked all the
other chaps to take off their hats to show her we were all the
same. She said she would write to our CO. We travelled
through London by train, and as we passed through Kentish
Town in the early morning one of the chaps saw his mother
at the window letting up the blind. He shouted, "There's my
mum!" and called to her but she didn't see him. He never
heard the last of it.'

George and the rest of the new recruits arrived in
Boulogne and marched to the nearby St Martin's Camp,
where they spent the night. The next morning they were on
the move again, marching the twenty miles or so to Étaples.

'On our way we were suddenly halted on the road next to
an orchard,' he said. 'I could see troops for about a mile in
front of us. The order came, "in fours, left turn", and then
we heard chanting. It was a funeral with a priest walking out

front carrying a crucifix. The coffin was on a farm cart and the relations were following behind. As it passed them the troops all went into the orchard like a khaki wave. We took the opportunity to get loaded up with apples. No one said a word to us, only one old lady hit the men with a big stick.'

After a twelve-hour march, George arrived at Étaples, was greeted in what had become the customary 'welcome to the war' infestation and put through Étaples' infamous rigorous training regime.

'We got our first lice there,' said George, 'and I don't think I was free of them all the time I was in France. We had one hour of every drill: bayonet fighting, physical drill, squad drill – we never stopped running from morning to night. They made a man into a soldier in ten days there.'

Étaples was the main transport depot and training camp for the Western Front mainly due to its excellent transport links. It was enormous, the largest overseas military camp ever established by the British anywhere in the world. 'Etaps', as it was known to the Tommies, earned itself a certain notoriety among new recruits and experienced soldiers returning after medical treatment in Britain. Wilfred Owen referred to it as 'a kind of paddock where the beasts were kept before the shambles', going on to describe how the men there had a certain look about them, *'an incomprehensible look, which a man will never see in England; nor can it be seen in any battle, but only in Étaples. It was not despair, or terror, it was more terrible than terror, for it was a blindfold look, and without expression, like a dead rabbit's.'*

Étaples was also home to several military hospitals, hence the enormous cemetery that remains there to this day, and it also served as a huge supply depot. For most of the war it was too far behind the lines for the German guns and aircraft, but during the Spring Offensive of 1918 it came briefly within reach and an aerial bombing raid caused extensive damage to some of the hospitals, causing many casualties. For most of the war, however, Étaples was safe but utterly terrifying.

The regime was equally ruthless whether you were a raw recruit who barely knew one end of a rifle from the other or an old lag with a chest full of medals returning to battle after being wounded at the front. It was not a place that anyone wanted to stay longer than necessary – some wounded men even chose to return to the Front before their wounds had properly healed rather than put up with any more of the Étaples regime.

There is a widely held theory that Étaples was the epicentre of the Spanish Flu pandemic that began in 1918, and the strict regime at the camp triggered a serious mutiny in September 1917 as the army prepared for the Third Battle of Ypres. There had been numerous small incidents and injustices over time that had built up a gradual but steady tide of discontent among the men at the way they were treated. The returning soldiers in particular greatly resented their treatment at the hands of officers who, in the main, had never been any closer to the front than Étaples. However strict the discipline, however austere the authority of the camp commanders, it was inevitable that the situation would eventually come to a head. James Watson of the Northumberland Fusiliers had passed through in 1916 when the talk was of the belligerence of the military police, known as 'redcaps'.

'We'd arrived in Rouen and they took us away in cattle trucks with rails around the top,' he said. 'We travelled from the base to Etaps; there was the bull ring, all sand about a foot or more deep. There were bags full of straw attached to posts, and they were supposed to be Germans and we had to run up to them and stick the bayonet into them. The instructors were murder and when you were going or coming back to your billets there would always be military police around. You'd be marching along and if you happened to talk to somebody or look around, they'd shout at you.

'There was a place at Etaps where there was a railway line over a bridge. Over the other side was a part of town that was out of bounds to Tommies – only officers were allowed. It was where the red lamps were, the women. There were two redcaps posted at each end of the bridge and a Scottish soldier went one night. When he came back there was an argument, they got hold of him and threw him over the bridge.'

There are various versions of the story such as James Watson's above, many of which have clearly come at the end of a long game of Chinese whispers, but what seems to have occurred on 9 September 1917 was the arrest of a New Zealand soldier for desertion, when he was returning late from the town. This led a rowdy crowd of his colleagues to gather at the gates. Here a struggle broke out and a military policeman, Private Herbert Reed, opened fire, killing Cameron Highlander Corporal W. B. Wood. Discipline in the camp subsequently broke down for three whole days until order was fully restored. Many men were punished for their role in the incident, most severely Corporal Jesse Short of the Northumberland Fusiliers, who was executed.

Fred Dixon happened to be there at the time, having been transferred from the cavalry to the infantry and joining the 10th Queen's. He was no greenhorn by this time, though, having had a busy war up until 1917.

'We were transferred from cavalry to infantry because they were short of men. We'd all had combat experience, some of us at Gallipoli, some in the western desert, the Somme in 1916, then in 1917, when the Germans retired to the Hindenburg line, we were allowed to take our horses over the Somme and go and find them. After one patrol the officer told me afterwards that we had advanced further towards St-Quentin than anyone until the later stages of the war. Two of our squadron won the Military Medal for that patrol. So, we had plenty of combat experience. We were typical of chaps who'd been wounded, sent home to England and come back to re-join their units, but when they got back to Etaps found that the discipline was literally Prussian. After three years of war these troops were in no mood to be messed about by base wallahs who had never even been to the front.

'The bull ring was where were to be transferred from the cavalry to infantry. We'd be worked morning, noon and night by sergeant majors who wore yellow bands on their arms that earned them the nickname "canaries". At the end of each day, columns of us would be waiting to be released from the bull ring. There was a rostrum where a colonel inspected every detachment that passed, and if he didn't like the way you were marching you were sent to the back like a naughty schoolboy. Being cavalry men we weren't used to marching so this would happen to us quite often.

'At midday we used to march back from the bull ring and have a meal then march back again afterwards. Lady Angela Forbes ran the canteen at Étaples at the time, and she introduced some wooden huts up at the bull ring so the troops could have a cold meal of bully there instead of having to march all the way back to camp just to eat. It was very kind, but she didn't realise that we wouldn't be allowed to make use of the time saved – they just introduced extra drills. This kind of discontent smouldered and it only needed a spark to touch the whole thing off. However, by no means was the Étaples disturbance a mutiny, not even in the sense of the *Oxford Dictionary*. The troops were simply lawless and it was a riot, a prolonged riot. The town of Étaples was out of bounds; nobody was allowed there without a pass and the route lay over a railway bridge guarded by redcaps. The redcaps were not looked upon with favour at the time. Lady Forbes said in her book that the redcaps copied the manner of the Acting Brigade Major who was disliked by all and sundry. I think his name was Strahan. One afternoon, a Jock wanted to go into town but hadn't got a pass. The redcap told him he couldn't go. The Jock insisted, the redcap insisted. There was an argument, a skirmish, and the redcap pulled out his revolver and shot the Jock dead. That was enough for the Scots. In the depots at Étaples were Imperial troops: English, Welsh, Scots Irish, Canadians, Aussies and New Zealanders, so then the Australians joined in because they resisted any type of imperial discipline. Then the Canadians became involved and before long the whole town was alight, ablaze with rioting troops. All law and order disappeared and shots were fired. The major in charge of our Queen's infantry base depot stood on a box and said to us, "Please don't go down to the town tonight, boys."

'We didn't go, but even we were affected by the atmosphere. About an hour later we were paraded with trenching tools and topcoats and marched down to the bull ring. The next morning at daybreak we were marched back again and got down between the blankets. At six in the morning, "Reveille" sounded and the sergeant was hitting the tents, shouting "Show a leg". Normally we would have done – reluctantly, but we would have done as we were told, even though it was unfair. On that morning, though, someone called out something unrepeatable at him and we didn't show a leg. The same thing happened half an hour later and we finally got our breakfast about 9 o'clock and nothing more was said. All the redcaps had gone from near us, but on the rare occasions when they were around they were in groups about twenty strong.'

It wasn't all grimness at Étaples, though, and it seems at least one of the sergeants wasn't hell bent on harsh discipline and ritual humiliation.

'On one occasion we were taken in hand by a cockney sergeant wearing a VC ribbon,' said Fred. 'He marched us out to the sand dunes and we fell out, sat down and he said in his cockney accent, "Nah, ah'm going to give you a talk on *spirit dee corpse*. If you was in the canteen and I came in and you said, 'What will you 'ave, sergeant?' that's *spirit dee corpse*. Right, lads, now you can smoke." And that was it; that talk was supposed to last half an hour.'

If Edward had travelled to Flanders via Étaples, which is likely, the chances are that Alan Short was there at the same time, as he arrived at the camp with his regiment four days after Edward had made his will. They may even have crossed the Channel together.

'Off I went on 5 April 1918 with my whole company, all 213 of us,' said Alan. 'We marched down to Sheerness station, changed at Gillingham or somewhere, and carried on to Folkestone. We got there about midnight and slept on the floor of some old houses on the Leas, and then the next morning we were on the boat from Folkestone to Boulogne. It was a smooth crossing but half the fellas were seasick. I wasn't. The first impression I had of France was of a long wooden jetty and a solitary English girl in uniform standing at the end looking out to sea. Then we were on the docks and there was some officer directing us, giving orders. There were so many English people there it didn't feel like being in France. We were marched up St Martin's Hill where we saw some French boys selling tomatoes. I bought one, but it was damned expensive at tuppence ha'penny, the dearest tomato I think I ever bought.

'At St Martin's we were put in lorries and shipped off with thirty or forty men to another lorry, along straight narrow roads with poplar trees in avenues. I didn't know where we were going and didn't really care: we were just in France. Back in England I'd felt a sort of shiver, a funny feeling wondering whether I'd be all right. I was as worried about being scared as I was about being killed. But now we were here I didn't really feel anything. We spent the night in a camp somewhere, then entrained to Abbeville, then along the coast from Boulogne to Étaples.'

If being in France had somehow eased his fears, Alan's early tasks at Étaples couldn't have been better designed to remind him of his own mortality: 'One day we were sent on burial fatigue. There was a large cemetery at Étaples and thousands of men were buried there. They'd all been brought to the hospitals there and died of their wounds. We used to bring them from the mortuary of the 69th Canadian General Hospital on a two-wheeled stretcher to the cemetery. There was a parson and a bugler who blew the "Last Post", and this would go on day after day. We used to take turns fetching the bodies and filling in the graves. I suppose it was a way of breaking us in for what was to come.

'I was seventeen years old and already I was well acquainted with death.'

10

'THOUGH MANY BRAVE UNWRITTEN TALES, WERE SIMPLY TOLD IN VAPOUR TRAILS'

When I walked through the same Folkestone streets that had seemed so forbidding the previous night a miraculous transformation appeared to have taken place. The sun shone through the chill on a bright, cloudless spring morning and onto streets filling with happy shoppers, bleaching the austere, empty darkness of the evening into a tangible cheeriness.

I was heading east to Dover which, given I just had to head for the sea and turn left, ensured that even I couldn't possibly get lost. I descended the zigzag path down the cliff to sea level – a path originally constructed in the nineteenth century to facilitate the passage of bath chairs from hotels to the seafront, and reinforced in the 1920s with Pulhamite, a surprisingly effective form of artificial rock that seemed from its appearance to be made from any old rubble and junk, and whose recipe died with its creator – but soon realised that I probably needed to be back on the top. Thankfully, I discovered the Leas Lift, a funicular railway dating back to 1885, fuelled by nothing more refined than water.

I paid my £1 fare and sat in the carriage waiting to ascend, when I was joined by two middle-aged men, apparently friends on holiday. One was tall, wearing a cagoule and carrying a shopping bag, the other small with slicked-back hair and a copy of the *Racing Post* sticking out of the pocket of his checked sports jacket. His name was Dave. I knew this because his friend didn't stop talking to him and addressing him by name from the moment they arrived to the moment they left.

'Ooh, look, I see the fare's gone up today, Dave, look it says so on the notice, Dave, we should have come yesterday, Dave, before it went up, Dave, I said yesterday we should go up, Dave, didn't I, Dave, wish we had, Dave, we'll be off any second, won't we, Dave, shouldn't take long, Dave, have you still got those boiled sweets, Dave, we might need one in case our ears pop, eh, Dave, ha, I'm only joking, Dave …'

And so on … for the entire ascent. Dave didn't get a single word in all the way up. Come to think of it, his name probably wasn't even Dave – he's just never had the chance to say so.

I continued east along streets filling up with people, the spring weather having put everyone in a chipper mood and brought them outside. That night Manchester United were playing Bayern Munich: Folkestone's legacy of being the front line for two wars was effectively summed up by a blackboard outside a pub advertising simply 'Manchester United v Germans'. Further on I came to the town's small fishing harbour. From behind the shutters of one of the seafood shops came the gravelly cascade of that morning's whelk catch being delivered, while from the harbour itself there came the throaty diesel chuckle of a fishing boat starting its engines. A seafood stall opened its shutters as I passed, its painted sign informing: 'Opening hours subject to sea conditions and hangovers.'

It was a marvellous scene in the sunshine and I sat there for a while, tempted by a pot of jellied eels from the hangover man but deciding it was too soon after breakfast. Eels or no eels, I was reluctant to leave this glorious transformed Folkestone, but hauled on my pack and set off again. I rounded the end of the harbour and commenced a steep climb up to the top of the cliffs – so steep I sometimes felt I was in danger of grazing my nose on the ground in front of me. Halfway up I paused for breath, turned round and saw the fishing boat I'd seen earlier heading into the Channel haze towards an invisible horizon, a grey silhouette at the point of a wide wake on the calm water as a noisy gang of seagulls whirled overhead.

I continued a long, steep and sweaty climb past a Martello tower to the top of the cliffs. I'd hoped to be able to see France, but the sun was struggling to burn off the haze and once up on top I could barely see Folkestone, let alone anywhere further afield.

The path passed along an occasionally unsettlingly narrow gap between the caravan parks and the cliff edge, and my legs were still trembling from the combination of climb and vertigo when I happened upon the Battle of Britain monument at Capel-le-Ferne. I must confess I'd never even heard of it before, but I was soon mightily impressed. It's a place of evocative simplicity: three stone paths converge on a central point forming a propeller when viewed from the sky. At the centre is a plain statue of a young man in a flying jacket, sitting with his arms around his knees and looking out towards France.

Behind him a memorial wall lists the names of everyone who flew in the Battle of Britain, Churchill's 'few', all 2,936 of them. Replicas of a Spitfire and a Hurricane stand nearby next to the small café, where I sat with a cup of tea, looked out to sea and replayed in my mind a couplet from the poem 'Our Wall' by RAF veteran William Walker – who died in 2012, a few months shy of his one-hundredth birthday – which adorns a small plaque next to the memorial: 'Though many brave unwritten tales, were simply told in vapour trails'. Sitting there in the sunshine, I thought about how these lines summed up what I was looking for in pursuing Edward's story. Each of us has an Edward Connelly in our family history, an ordinary fellow thrust into the most extraordinary circumstances, a man who would have seen remarkable things and been a part of remarkable events. I was attempting to coax Edward from the mists of time, but so far all I'd achieved was a one-dimensional framework of a life, a stark basis of cold facts on which the first-hand stories and recollections would never hang. The collective silence of many of the returning men, unwilling or unable to relive the trauma, has meant that it wasn't just the dead whose stories were lost. Countless brave, unwritten tales lie forever undiscovered among the criss-crossing vapour trails of history.

I pressed on over the cliffs until eventually the silhouette of Dover Castle appeared on the horizon. The castle was, among other things, the target of the first bomb ever to be dropped on Britain. It was Christmas Eve 1914, and while the famous truce was underway on a section of the Western Front a German FF29 aircraft was circling Dover looking for a target. Its pilot was 26-year-old Stefan von Prondzynski, and when he saw the castle and the adjacent naval dockyard he picked up a bomb and heaved it over the side of his plane. He missed his intended targets, and the bomb landed instead in a rectory garden, causing nothing more disturbing than a crater in the lawn, some broken windows and a startled gardener to fall out of a tree.

Over the centuries Dover has seen countless millions of people come into and out of the country, for reasons good and bad, and exciting and frightening. It's a place anchored in our history by its very transience. I spent my final evening in England before departing for Flanders dining at the ancient White Horse Inn, to which cross-channel swimmers descend after completing – or in some cases not completing – their crossings. The walls are covered with signatures, considerably more of them than when I'd last visited a decade earlier, and it's a sobering reminder of just how close this stretch of the coastline is to France. I read a few of the inscriptions while sipping a pint and waiting for my whitebait. Having crossed from England to France in thirteen hours, one recent swimmer had also managed seven hours in the return direction before abandoning the attempt. 'Failure I can handle,' he wrote, 'but I couldn't handle not trying.'

When I turned the light out that night I lay awake with a strange apprehension hanging over me. I've done a reasonable amount of long-distance walking in my time but never outside Britain and Ireland. I had an itinerary and a couple of decent maps, and I was well equipped and prepared. There really wasn't much to worry about. If I was nervous ahead of the next day's crossing, one can only imagine what young lads like Edward were thinking the night before their departure. They were boys who, in many cases, had never ventured further than the streets surrounding their homes, schools and places of work, let alone out of the country. There was me, wondering whether I'd remember that cars came from the other direction when I crossed the road, while Edward and his equivalents were spending their last night in England before being herded onto a boat with hundreds of other new recruits all wondering whether they'd ever see Britain again and trying not to think too hard about what lay ahead of them.

11

'WHEN WE GOT TO HIM ALL HIS INSIDES WERE OUT. HE HAD A GIRL'S FACE. HE WAS EVER SO YOUNG'

Most of the new recruits would remain at Étaples or its equivalent for around ten days, at which point the men would be divided into companies and sent to the front line. The division was done with scant thought for the men involved, meaning that the new recruits would often be thrown into a group with complete strangers and separated from the men they'd trained with and come to know. 'They did it in alphabetical order so we lost some of our mates,' recalled George Fortune. 'That was the way they used to do things, really rough.'

The men would travel to the front by a combination of rail and marching. The train journeys were awful: the French rail network had not been as advanced as Britain's even before the war, and certainly not now that France was a war zone. The men would be crammed in with no facilities and many would pass eye-rolling comment on the sign painted onto the trucks, '40 hommes, 8 chevaux'. Forty men or eight horses. There was rarely seating, for these were trucks normally used for moving livestock with all their attendant residue, stains and smells. The men would lie or sit if they could, hanging their packs from nails on the walls, but often there wouldn't even be room to sit down.

The carriages would be sweltering and stinking in the summer, and freezing cold in the winter. Invariably the roofs – some men were even transported in open carriages – would leak. The journeys were painfully slow, too. The twenty-mile ride between Boulogne and Étaples, for example, could take three hours by train. Toilet breaks had to be taken during the train's frequent stops, when it was also sometimes possible to make tea from boiling water in the engine. Revolting though the conditions were, the men were by now becoming used to the lower expectations of comfort, hygiene and sanitation that came with being a soldier. They also knew there was worse to come when they got to the Front.

'Off to the Front we went, about three days in open cattle trucks,' remembered George Fortune. 'When we went through a town or a village the children would run alongside and call out, "Bully beef, bis-kweets Jock!" We didn't have a biscuit between us as we had lost our rations when we'd changed trains and went about three days without grub. I ate my iron rations, which consisted of a small tin of corned beef and a biscuit which you were not allowed to eat without permission from an officer. We spent days in those cattle trucks. Sometimes horses had been in there before us – and we used to smell of horses for days after lying on the wet floor. We were well and truly lousy now and used to spend a lot of time "chatting", as we called it. We would squash them between our thumbnails. The seams of our trousers and shirts were lined with nits – we used to crack them before they came to life. Water was only for drinking: the only way we could have a wash was if we came across a river or stream. Our bodies all had broken skin where we'd been scratching ourselves in our sleep.'

Wilfred Heavens of the London Irish Rifles was making a similar rail journey around the time Edward would have been making his way to the front for the first time in April 1918. Wilfred was from Hammersmith, not far from Edward's part of London, and was the son of a furniture shop manager; he had joined up in 1914 at the age of eighteen.

'During the night there was a fall of snow and it was bitterly cold inside the trucks,' he wrote. 'Just after midnight the train came to a standstill and we were informed we could get some tea from a marquee in a field on the side of a railway track. We climbed out and after walking practically the whole length of the train, crossed the tracks, jumped a ditch and climbed through a wire fence where we eventually found the marquee. What with it being dark, the ground slippery with frost and the wind terribly cold, we wondered after we had started whether it was worthwhile, but did not like giving up after going so far. Chaps were slipping over and some returning with tea in their mess tins tripped over and spilt it all. The language heard on all sides was rather choice. On arriving at the marquee we managed to get some tea, though it was not much. After hunting about trying to find the truck we had left, we got there minus a good drop of tea. I put my mess tin on the floor of the truck and started to climb in, slipped, made a grab and knocked over the mess tin with the remainder of the tea.

Why we did not drink it as soon as we received it, I do not know. Towards morning frost appeared on the inside of the truck.'

The men would have become more used to marching at this stage, but it was still a deeply unpleasant ordeal. Their packs could weigh anything up to 65lb and they were marched in all weathers, from searing heat to torrential downpours and even in snow. What made marching in France and Flanders even harder was that many of the roads were cobbled rather than tarmacked. In bad weather the mud on the roads could sometimes be deep enough to seep over the top of the men's boots. For all its discomforts, the train was still far more preferable to the road.

At the end of this ordeal of train and marching which, depending on where you were going and the prevalent conditions, could take many days, the new recruits finally arrived at the war. They'd had the civilian marched and drilled out of them, they'd been herded to the front like cattle and they were now simply soldiers. A name, a rank and a number, part of a massive, dehumanised machine whose movements were dictated by men with elaborate moustaches gathered with their hands clasped behind their backs around maps in châteaux across the region. I tried to picture Edward, a pale face viewed through the slats of a cattle truck somewhere in France, gazing sightlessly out into the night, or pounding along a rural road in the rain, head down, feeling each and every cobble through the soles of his boots, every blister zinging, desperate to claw at the itchiness of the lice already infesting every recess of his uniform.

Arriving at the Front must have been like arriving on a different planet: the trenches, the dugouts, the sandbags, the barbed wire, the landscape blasted and obliterated by nearly four years of constant battering. How much of it would he have taken in? How inured to hardship would his weeks of training and drilling and marching have made him? What were his first impressions of arriving at the Front?

At the end of his long train journey, George Fortune climbed down from the cattle trucks cold, aching and hungry near Ypres. The battalion immediately fell in.

'Our CO inspected us,' he recalled, 'and said, "Not bad, but not much guts in you. You wait till you see my men when they come out of the line." We expected to see great big fellows but they were bantams, little fellows. They were really tough men, though. Most were miners. They were a good lot of men. They had been in and out of the line for sixteen months and were due a rest.'

Horace Calvert arrived in Poperinge, Flanders, in April 1916 to be immediately placed in a platoon in Number 3 Company: 'I was the only newcomer in that platoon. They were billeted in a store for horse-drawn carts in the town square when I arrived, and as I was the last one to go in I got the outside. It was a stone floor, I had a greatcoat, no blanket, and that's how I had to sleep. It was a very uncomfortable night and I didn't sleep. The other men gave me a lot of knowledge as to what to expect up the line: keep your head down, never stand up in the open, take as much food as you can get hold of with you, and cigarettes if you're a smoker. And take as much water as you can carry. We went along a road which went through the German lines then turned off across open fields. It was pitch black and when I stopped to make sure the direction was right there were Verey lights going up and I thought we were surrounded. After a lot of hard walking – the ground was terrible, all shell holes more or less – slipping and sliding, carrying water, sandbags, ammunition, as well as my own pack, eventually we got to the trenches.'

On arriving at his post for the first time, Horace's battalion relieved the Scots Guards and he was immediately put on sentry duty. He took his place on the firing step, placed his rifle muzzle into the aperture between sandbags and squinted into no man's land towards the German lines ahead.

'The sergeant said to me, "All you've got to do is stand still, look out and if you see any movement, unless you've been told otherwise, fire,"' Horace remembered. 'There was a smell of death all around. I mentioned the smell and they told me this ground had been fought over so many times and there were so many dead that the smell of it was in the soil.'

If the smell of death was all-pervasive, the complete absence of personal hygiene in the front lines ensured that it was mixed with all sorts of other unpleasant aromas to create a bouquet of almost feral humanity.

'Conditions were rudimentary to say the least,' recalled Horace. 'A latrine pit was dug about six-feet deep with a pole across it for you to sit on, and you'd throw soil on it when you finished. A lot of chaps were killed there, actually; they'd take their kit off and have a stretch but the German snipers were watching all the time.'

Even the act of arching the back to loop braces off the shoulders ready to drop one's trousers could be enough to give a sniper a sighting that would prove fatal. Not the most glamorous death in a world of unglamorous deaths. Even if you managed to do your bit of business without being killed, washing your hands afterwards was out of the question.

'You never washed from the time you went into the front line to when you got back,' said Horace. 'Your hands might have been in all sorts of things but you couldn't wash. Also, there were other things to bother about than dirty hands. You picked up lice as soon as you joined the battalion because all the other chaps had them. You couldn't cope with them, the irritation, running round the back of your neck, your armpits, your private parts. They bred quicker than you could kill them and you were itching all the time, which could be awkward on parade. As soon as you were out of the line you'd take your shirt and underwear off, take a candle, put it under a tin and burn them out, picking them off with your fingers. But you just couldn't keep pace with it.'

As Horace had found when he'd reached Étaples, soldiers would contract lice almost as soon as they arrived from England. They were a constant source of discomfort for everybody; in all the accounts of life on the Western Front, the two constant refrains throughout are death and lice. There were other irritations too: in the trenches, rats were another unwelcome and persistent form of fauna.

'We were instructed to bury rubbish, but some chaps would throw their tins over into no man's land and that's where we got trouble with the rats,' Horace recalled. 'When we went to the original front line trench at Ypres a lot of empty tins had been thrown over, which meant there were rats roaming around. So I got some pork out of a tin of beans and stuck it on the end of the bayonet. Then you'd point your rifle towards the Germans and when a rat came up you'd fire, hopefully killing the rat and maybe hitting a German. The rats were a very big nuisance. You had to watch your food or they'd be in your haversack. If anybody had to be buried, it wasn't long before you could see where the rats had been at each end of the grave, getting at the body. That wouldn't go down well if it was one of your pals you'd just buried.'

The constant presence of death, both its threat and the very real evidence all around, was something to which the recruits had to quickly adapt: 'Bodies were just loosely buried anywhere, and you'd put a cross up if you could. Shellfire would often disturb bodies but you had to ignore that. The smell would be shocking and seemed to cling to everything you had; you could even taste it in your food. It was a nasty sickly smell that you never forgot.'

Fred Baldwin, a teenage stretcher-bearer, recalled how there was little time or opportunity for any kind of dignified send-off for dead soldiers.

'Dead men were buried in a blanket,' he remembered. 'The padre would take a note of their particulars, going round the corpses and taking notes in order to write home to their people, then they were buried in shell holes tied up in a blanket. That's all we could do, drop them in a hole. There was no decorum.'

Horace had only been at the front for three nights when the full, close-up horror of the war came visiting: 'There was a German raid on the next company. I couldn't see anything but I heard the bombs going off, the rifle fire and the shouting. I've never forgotten the name of the first man I saw killed: Lieutenant McAleer, it was. He was leading a bombing party to go at some Germans who'd got behind the trench and were attacking from behind. I heard him call out "Bring the bombs" only for the Germans to give him one and blow half his face off. He was the first dead man I'd ever seen.'

Horace's unit lost twenty-three men in that particular raid. When word passed around the trench that a retaliatory raid was being prepared, sixty men volunteered for it.

'Just before they went I was sitting on the firing step with my rifle talking to a chap called Millichamp,' Horace recalled. 'He was one of those quiet kinds of Englishmen. I knew nothing about him but I'd talked to him quite a lot. He was about fifteen years older than me and I didn't know anything about him, no one did. He said to me, "I'll have a smoke before I go over," and pulled out his little clay pipe. But the stalk had broken so he couldn't have his smoke.'

The party set off into the darkness of no man's land and Horace was among those left in the trench watching anxiously from the firing step: 'Within minutes there was all hell being let loose over in the German trench, bombs, machine guns, rifles, the lot. The party came back carrying a lot of wounded and a few didn't come back, including Millichamp. According to another chap he'd been so badly wounded they couldn't move him. Later on, two officers went out to find him but he'd gone, and a couple of weeks later we found out that he'd died as a prisoner of war. I missed him quite a lot; I could talk to him. He was from the Midlands and would tell you all about Birmingham, but nobody knew if he was married or had a family because he told us nothing about himself. Maybe that was why he was so well-liked: he didn't ask anything of or about you, or tell you anything concerning himself. He was a nice man.'

Despite having endured what appeared to be almost a literal baptism of fire, Horace didn't seem to feel particularly frightened by his early experiences in the trench. It was, after all, what he'd signed up for.

'I looked upon it as a great adventure,' he said. 'I never gave any thought to danger. I thought I was being well protected one way or another, and it didn't strike me at all. Morale was good. There was a lot of leg-pulling and joking, and life was actually as happy as possible.'

In a few weeks Horace had gone from a boy in West Yorkshire learning to be an engineer and reading magazine adventure stories at the library to a soldier, scratching at lice and shooting at rats, going to the toilet in a muddy hole in the ground and apparently feeling no great sense of fear in the face of the constant threat and presence of death all around him. It had been a lightning-fast transformation that was common to all these men. James Watson, for example, found he'd adapted to trench life without even realising it.

'Belgium's a watery country,' he said, 'damp, musty, and nearly half of the duckboards would be broken. You were up to your knees in water and you just had to go on. In the dugouts you just had a sheet of corrugated iron over your head between you and the shells, and you thought you were safe!'

Whether it was a blasé attitude to danger or just getting too used to the way of life at the Front, James saw some needless tragedies: 'Some of the lads in the trenches, you couldn't drive sense into them. They'd smoke, you see, and the Germans would see there was somebody there smoking and a lot got killed because of that. There was a time I went home on leave and we gathered at the railway for a train of four or five trucks in the dark, all men going on leave. One fella was smoking and I said, "You want to put that cigarette out, mate," and just as he was getting out of the truck a bullet shot him dead: the red tip of his cigarette had given him away. I saw some awful sights like that. It was that bad in the trenches sometimes that they used to take their puttees off, wrap them round their toes and fire their rifles into their feet – self-inflicted, they'd do anything to get out of there. A "blighty wound", they called it, as it was enough to see you sent home for treatment. Some lads crippled themselves for life that way. I was in some tight corners at times but I never thought of doing anything like that.'

Thomas Park of the Middlesex Regiment was the same age as Edward and grew up not far away from Kensal Town, in Edgware. He'd spent the early part of the war working in a munitions factory, which initially excused him from joining up, but at the beginning of 1918 he and four friends from the factory decided to enlist. His father was already at the front as a driver and his mother had recently died, and when he told his boss at the factory he was joining up, he was told that in the circumstances he didn't have to go. Thomas was insistent.

'You got the casualty lists and read of the different battles in the papers. You got a lot of stories of German atrocities: they used to take a baby from a woman, kill the baby, rape the woman and then kill her, all that kind of propaganda. It made you want to get out there more; you took notice of it. We just wanted to go. We didn't realise what it was like, though. They talk about land of hope and glory and all that, but it's nothing like that when you're out there. I hadn't realised what they were going through out there. You read the papers but didn't have any idea what it was like.'

It wasn't long after arriving at the Front that Thomas, still a teenager, learned exactly what it was like when he was sent out as part of a raid on the German trenches. The accepted routine was that the artillery would send over a creeping barrage, a carefully timed artillery assault that moved forward to keep the shells the same distance ahead of the advancing troops, and the infantry would follow behind, ready to attack any Germans left behind after the barrage.

'When we got to France, we were marched up past the guns and were immediately aware of the smell of cordite. The whole thing was a different atmosphere altogether, your eyes ran and everything happened in the dark. We were told the barrage would go up, the tanks would be on our left and we were to take a salient. The barrage began, off we went and soon had a lot of casualties: I think we must have gone too fast and met our own barrage. When we did reach the trenches there were only three Germans there, one we killed and two we took prisoner, so the casualties we had could only have been from our own barrage.

'The German we killed, it was his own fault. He was only a young boy, about eighteen, I suppose, and we went in pointing revolvers at him, but instead of putting his hands up he suddenly stood up in the trench and our Lewis gunner got him in the stomach. When we got to him all his insides were out. He had a girl's face. He was ever so young. Then we got to a dugout and these two Germans came out, smoking cigars. Old guys they were. They gave themselves up.

'We'd only been in France about three or four days at this point. It was all happy go lucky; we were all about the same age, all Londoners, and we palled up. The atmosphere was quite light-hearted: one day we were walking up to the line and shells were coming over when one of our chaps said, "Here, somebody'll get hurt in a minute." I can't say I was actually afraid. Maybe a little bit, but generally I don't think I was. We'd only had three weeks' training but I could fire all right, and we all thought we could do our bit. Actually, there was a scary time once, when we had to go up from our trench at night and take a forward position. We went over the top and you were falling over chaps and you didn't know if they were dead or alive. Eventually we got to where we were going and relieved about four men who'd been holding this advanced position. It was an outpost, a horseshoe trench, and the Germans were very close. The barbed wire in front of the position had tins hanging on it and one of the men we were relieving said, "If you hear the tins rattle it's a German raid." Of course, as he's saying this we heard a tin rattle. Naturally we were scared for a moment, thinking the Germans were about to come over the top of us, but it turned out to be just a rat.'

When he arrived at the front, Victor Fagence's early experiences bred a confidence that might have surprised his civilian self. It was one that almost backfired on him, too.

He'd come through Messines in 1917, and in the spring of 1918 was preparing for another advance.

'This was my second experience of a major advance and I was less apprehensive this time,' he recalled. 'I had the foolish feeling that, having got through the Battle of Messines all right after being in danger of being killed a number of times, I was leading a charmed life.'

The terrain the troops had to cross was swampy with water-filled craters, and it had been raining constantly for days. Victor got ready to go by climbing over the top and lying on one of the white tapes laid by working parties, which directed advancing soldiers to the gaps cut in the barbed wire. The order to attack came at 0350.

'While we were lying on the tapes there was some shell-fire,' Victor said, 'and some men were wounded and probably killed – we heard screams. At first we came under fire, and as we advanced a bit further we found most of the enemy rifle and machine-gun fire ceased. Visibility wasn't good for either side, but once we started advancing the enemy engaged in moving his field guns further back.

'One of the Germans threw a stick bomb at me; I saw it coming, flung myself to the ground and it landed about four feet in front of me. I was all right, but the explosion meant I became separated from the rest of my team and ran off to the right flank to take stock of my position in a wooden shed I saw there. Once inside I realised that the best thing I could do from there was line up my Lewis gun at the enemy pillbox ahead and see if I could knock him out. I lined up the gun, pressed the trigger and the damn thing stopped straight away. It wasn't an easy thing to rectify: I found that the magazine was plastered up with mud and I had no cleaning rag with me. Then I realised that I had no rifle either, as the man carrying the spare parts bag for the Lewis gun, from whom I was now separated, had my rifle as well as his own.

'After a time I thought I'd better try and make my way back to rejoin some of the other men. I stood up, had a look round, and the battlefield appeared almost deserted. Then I saw a shallow with some of our men in it about eighty yards in front of the pillbox, so I set off towards them carrying my Lewis gun. When I got nearer to them a corporal shouted, "Get down, you bloody fool, you'll get killed," but I didn't think this German gunner would trouble himself to fire at me as he was firing in another direction at the time. When I got to the edge of the shell hole, however, he turned his gun round on to me. The next thing I knew I could feel bullets hitting the gun at waist height, then pains in my hands, a pain in my stomach, and I half-jumped, half-fell into the shell hole. When I landed I found blood running freely from my right hand. There happened to be a stretcher-bearer in the shell hole and he put a dressing on my hands, asking if I'd been hit anywhere else. I said in the stomach, I think. We undid my clothing and there was a hole on the right-hand side but it just felt like someone had punched or kicked me, so I thought it couldn't have done much damage.'

Victor managed to make his way to a dressing station half a mile away, where he found he was just one among a large number of wounded men arriving. There was no triage system so everyone was seen in order of arrival, no matter how serious or superficial their wounds. From there Victor and the rest of the walking wounded had to cross the

Ypres–Comines canal to some GS wagons, which carried them to Knokke, on the Franco-Belgian border, and then it was a train back to the coast and back to England. At the end of the journey, Victor found himself in a hospital near Stratford-upon-Avon.

William Dann first arrived in France in September 1915. He'd trained as a Lewis machine-gunner and was kept back for an extra week behind the rest of his battalion for more firing practice, before rejoining the 10th Queen's in the Passchendaele sector. As a newcomer to the battlefield, he didn't expect to be selected for any raids or attacks for a while.

'The front line was in Passchendaele,' remembered William, 'which used to be a village but was all blown to bits by the time we got there. Under cover of night we went up to the entrance of Poppy Lane, which was a mile-long communications trench that led up to Passchendaele, and there we were, at the front line, with the Germans ahead of us to the right on the ridge. During that first night there was a lull in the gunfire and we heard rumours we were going over the top. I thought, surely they want more experienced men than us; we've only just got here. But it was true: we were going over the top. The officer came round with a tot of rum, strong stuff, the first time I'd ever had it, and told us we were going over at dawn. Not only that, us Lewis gunners had to be the first over to set up our guns for covering fire.

'When the time came we went over and crept along the ground to the best spot we could find to provide covering fire. Of course, the Germans realised straight away that something was happening and opened up a terrific barrage. You couldn't hear a thing – you had to use hand and arm signals, couldn't even begin to hear anything. There were shells bursting everywhere, machine guns, small arms, mortars, it was terrible; I'd never known anything like it.'

No amount of training could have prepared William for this. With five in his team – his number two and four lads carrying ammunition – he and his colleagues found themselves barely twenty-five yards from the German trench: 'All you could see was their men struggling the same as we were. Eventually they did break and started going back to their own lines, but the barrage was still going on. It was very dirty and muddy and we had an awful job getting about because we had to crawl in it, keeping low. It had rained as we were going up Poppy Lane and eased off when we went over the top in the morning, but the mud was awful. When daylight broke it wasn't a good sight to see, dead and wounded men lying about everywhere. They were moaning, some of them, but what could you do? There wasn't anything you could do. Eventually the stretcher-bearers would come and the dead and wounded would be taken away, but we were powerless to help. The artillery would have to die down eventually to let the guns cool down, and that's when the stretcher-bearers could come out. There was an unwritten wartime rule about a lull to pick up the dead and wounded, but there was still some firing and shelling at different times as they did so.'

To give an idea of just how many dead and wounded there were on the battlefield that morning, not to mention how lucky William was to come back alive, let alone unscathed, where his battalion had had a full complement of 1,000 men, he was the last of just fifty-two to make it back to the trenches.

'Fifty-two. That tells you what sort of slaughter it was,' he said. 'Luckily, I came out of it and got back to Passchendaele, but three of my gun team were hit. I can't say I wasn't scared. I'd never experienced anything like it before, of course, and when the barrage went up it made you even more scared. But when you're under a heavy barrage your nerves get used to it and you don't take so much notice. You know you might be killed and never come back, but that sort of thing you don't think about, or at least you shouldn't do. I didn't.'

Within days of his arrival in the lines, William Dann had already been through the worst of the Western Front. Almost immediately he'd become used to the vagaries of life on the front line, both in the devastating action outlined above and also in the routines and rhythms of the everyday: 'We came back into Passchendaele to our front line and just held that line. We were there for an eight-day stretch, then you'd go back into a reserve trench until the other chaps who'd relieve you did their eight days, and up you'd go again until there was another advance or raid. Shells were always flying over, day and night, from some angle. We were getting casualties just the same. When we came out of the line we'd go to the cellars in Ypres for a rest. We'd lay there and you could see rats running over your feet, the cellars were full of them. We were riddled with lice, too, but you couldn't get a bath. The only thing you could do was if you happened to be out of the line on a sunny day you could take your shirt off and go through the seams cracking the lice. You'd call them greybacks. If you laid your clothes out in the sun it would bring them out, you could see them.'

He'd also soon become used to the alien world and land-scape of the front, with its blasted trees, cloying mud and a vista completely dominated by shell holes: 'It was kind of a wilderness, us chaps on both sides and all the gunfire going back and forth. That was it. No birds, no insects, nothing, just the sound of artillery. You couldn't get washed, either, beyond sloshing a bit of trapped rainwater over your face if you could find some. You could go three months without a bath: the most comfortable bath I had was after six months at the Front, back at Steenvoorde. Life wasn't pleasant. The sanitary business in the front line was awful, well, you got no sanitaries at all. You'd dig a little hole in the corner or you'd take a shovel and sling it over the top. Food-wise you'd get these big army billy cans with some kind of soup that was quite good for the conditions we were under. Later on, they couldn't get fresh water to wash out the pots they'd made the soup in, and they had to make the tea in it, too, so your tea would taste of the soup.

'Spirits were generally good, though. Some of the chaps were very amiable and jokey, even in the front line, but they were older men, not us young chaps – we just stuck it out. They'd say, "They won't kill me, it's you young fellows they're after," and the next day they might be gone. Some men broke down. I saw one or two. I knew men later in the war who'd been in since 1914 and they'd still break down. One man shot his finger off, his trigger finger, at Passchendaele. He was hysterical and he did it on the spur of the moment. I don't know what happened to him.'

In late 1917, William Dann, by then a battle-hardened soldier despite being barely eighteen, and the 10th Queen's were holding a line just east of Ypres when the word came through that they were to make another advance.

'That was a wet night, miserable,' said William. 'I was lying on the trunk of a tree to get out of the mud, and eventually the advance started. I slithered off this trunk, picked up my gun and walked off, and suddenly I was knocked down flat – a bit of shrapnel knocked me out cold. I came round and there was an officer standing over me saying, "You all right, Bill?" I said, "No, I've got a burning feeling right in the back of my head." He had a look and said, "It's no good, you'll have to go back." He bandaged me up as best he could and asked if I could walk. I gave him the Lewis gun and struggled off back to the dressing station where they took me in and gave me a cold cup of cocoa to drink. It wasn't very good, but it was all they had.

'With the rest of the wounded I was moved off in a GS wagon to the nearest station, where there was an ambulance train to take us to a hospital deep inside France, and I was in there a couple of months because my wound wouldn't heal up. They said it was half of a shell cap from a gas shell that had hit me. It infected the flesh and it had to be scraped three times, but eventually it healed. They put us on a French farm for convalescence for twelve days. I remember it was autumn because we went apple picking, about a dozen of us.

'Then they sent us back to our base camp at Boulogne. When we got there we found that our battalion, the 10th Queen's, had been sent to the Italian front.'

12

'A BOY OF EIGHTEEN, LOOKING AROUND AT THE SEA OF FACES THAT SEEMED SO ASSURED'

Dover was still dark when I rose early to catch the ferry to Calais, but I still had to bustle along the marina in order to make it just before check-in closed. It was yet another hazy morning, and the white cliffs soon disappeared behind us as we ploughed out of the harbour and into the Channel. So achromatic was the post-dawn light that it was hard to tell where the cliffs ended and the sea and sky began. Countless thousands of troops had made this crossing during both wars, and for many the shrinking cliffs would have been their last-ever glimpse of their native home, the disappearing horizon behind them soon to be replaced by a new one ahead, one of barbed wire and sandbags.

I sat lulled by the low thrum of the engines in a lounge at the front of the ship, the near-white sun drawing an ever-shifting dazzle from the water. I waited for France to appear and once again thought about the khaki-clad thousands of a century before, their equipment familiar from their training but suddenly feeling lumpy and heavy in their hands, strange to their nervous fingering. They would be looking round at the strange faces and hearing the strange accents and wondering who, if any of them, would become friends, colleagues, life-savers; all of them shoring up the facade of a works outing with banter and quips, but all of them feeling the cold knot of fear deep in the pits of their stomachs.

I looked at my rucksack on the seat next to me: it contained everything I'd need – and a few things I wouldn't – for the next week or more, and suddenly looked hopelessly inadequate. I knew I'd be coming back – there was a Eurostar ticket in my bag to prove it – but Edward's crossing was open-ended; he didn't know how long he'd be gone or when he might see his family again. I tried to imagine him, a boy of eighteen, looking around at the sea of faces that seemed so assured, sucking on cigarettes, falling into easy conversations in accents he could barely understand. Everyone else, propped up by flimsy bravado, would have looked so assured, so confident, as if they did this all the time.

We were virtually in the harbour before the faint silhouette of the French coast emerged from the haze. Before I knew it we'd docked, disembarked and I was outside the passenger terminal, about to commence what was, for me, the most nerve-racking part of the journey: the bit I wasn't doing on foot. As a foot passenger you can't travel between the south coast and Belgium any more. Having based my original itinerary on travelling from Ramsgate to Ostend, I had discovered just too late that the route no longer runs. Dover to Ostend was also closed to me, as that route requires you to have a vehicle, even if it's a bicycle. Hence I was a long way west of where I needed to be and had needed to come up with a plan B: I'd take the bus from Calais to the border and walk from the Belgian coast to Diksmuide, then on to Poperinge, Ypres, Courtrai and finally to Edward's grave in the small town of Harelbeke, skirting along the coast before plunging into the heart of Flanders in a manoeuvre I liked to call 'the reverse Schlieffen'. As long as I walked from the coast I would still be making the complete journey on foot. And at least I didn't have to endure ten days at Étaples first.

I changed at Dunkirk and joined a commuter bus that would take me along the shoreline to De Panne, just over the Franco-Belgian border, from where I'd resume my walk. Sitting opposite me on the bus was possibly the politest man in the whole of France. He was determined to give up his seat to anyone, young or old, male or female. Everyone declined until I thought he might be reduced to shouting through the window and gesturing to passers-by that his seat was available if necessary. So wrapped up did he become in his own extreme selflessness that, in attempting to offer his seat to a man with a small dog, he almost forgot that we'd reached his stop and had to bolt for the doors before they closed.

The penultimate stop on the route was the evocatively named Plopsaland, a theme park inspired by Belgian children's TV characters such as Big & Betsy and Wizzy & Woppy. It had, since the 1930s and before the turn of the millennium, been a bee-themed establishment owned by a honey company, which sounds like it was a magnificent thing.

I alighted at De Panne railway station, part of a conurbation with Adinkerke, a border town which, thanks to the cheaper duty on cigarettes in Belgium than in France, boasts more tobacconists per capita than anywhere else in Europe. De Panne was part of a fiercely defended sliver of Belgium not conquered by the Germans during the First World War; hence it was home to the King and Queen of Belgium for most of the conflict. It was this line of defence behind which a small part of Belgium stayed defiantly Belgian that would comprise my next couple of days of walking.

I set off following a path alongside the Nieuwport–Ostend canal as far as Veurne then turned south-east across the countryside in the direction of Diksmuide. My first impressions of Flanders included the grateful realisation that it was as flat as if laid with a spirit level, which is always good news when you've a long way to walk. I passed by endless fields, farms and the occasional village, a flat horizon ahead of me save for the odd church spire and, on one occasion, a proper, old-fashioned windmill. There was something strange yet still familiar about the landscape, and then it struck me: this is what Kent would look like if someone grabbed it firmly by the coastline and yanked it flat.

Eventually, under the late-afternoon sun, I saw the thumping, Brutalist hammer head of Diksmuide's IJzertoren punching into the horizon ahead of me. At nearly 300 feet in height, the austere-looking First World War memorial dominates the skyline for miles around, the largest monument of its kind in Europe and one given extra presence by the flatness of the landscape.

I fixed my bearings on the tower and made for Diksmuide, passed through the outskirts of the town and came to its heart, the Grote Markt. Diksmuide began life in the twelfth century as a market town at the centre of the local agriculture industry before it was knocked about by the various northern European wars between the Middle Ages and the end of the eighteenth century, until, after a relatively quiet hundred years, Diksmuide found itself a defining node, both of the Western Front and of a particular sense of Belgian-ness. The River Yser passes through the town and continues south, a waterway that became the Belgian line for practically the duration of the war: while the Germans pushed through the rest of Belgium into France, they couldn't cross the Yser. It was the last Belgian frontier, mainly thanks to the locals flooding much of the region with seawater and making it impassable between here and Nieuwport on the coast, but also due to some incredibly brave and dogged resistance from the Belgian army. It was this courage and determination that gave birth to a renewed sense of Flemish identity in the region.

It had been a very long day that had begun in Dover and involved a ferry, two buses and a thirteen-mile walk. I slipped off my rucksack and flopped onto a bench in the Grote Markt, my feet throbbing and feeling every yard of the walk. While the flatness of the landscape was welcome from a walking point of view, the fact that I'd walked almost exclusively on roads and pavements meant that my feet had taken a pounding.

Almost before I knew it I'd sat in the square for the better part of an hour, but in that time I'd realised something that was going to define much of my time in the towns of West Flanders. I appeared to be sitting in an ancient cobbled square of buildings of various vintages, from the late medieval onwards. Most of the frontages were framed by typically Flemish roofs – steep, almost steepled – with step gables. They were tall and narrow, with elaborate windows, and ranged in age over hundreds of years.

Except they didn't. Like many towns in this epicentre of the fighting and shelling, Diksmuide was almost entirely destroyed between 1914 and 1918. At the end of the war there was barely a building standing, and in the Grote Markt where I was sitting was an expanse of rubble and twisted metal punctured by the odd stump of still-laid bricks, the only hint of the ancient and thriving town that had once stood here. Hundreds of years of social and economic development and architectural progress lay mixed up on the ground, the shattered buildings releasing their centuries-long historical narratives and countless human stories from destroyed rooms to scatter on the wind across the devastated landscape.

A couple of years after the end of the war, Diksmuide and towns like it made an extraordinary decision. They could have abandoned the place altogether. They could have swept away all the debris to plan and build an entirely new town. But no, they determined to faithfully reconstruct the town until it was exactly as it had been on the day war broke out in the summer of 1914: every building, every road, every detail. Hence, Diksmuide today is a wonderful piece of historical sleight-of-hand and a delightful middle finger to the bullying arrogance of blind destruction.

I sat on a bench outside the tourist office facing the town hall, currently undergoing renovations. Hung from the scaffolding on the front of the building was an artist's impression of how the building would look when the work is finished. Which, of course, is how it looked before the current renovations, and also how it looked before it was destroyed and rebuilt as good as new. This was about as literal an example of Diksmuide's many-layered nature as you could get.

It was very quiet in the square. There was the flap of the town-hall sheeting in the breeze, the occasional rumble of car wheels and rubbery slither of bicycle tyres on the cobbles, but otherwise Diksmuide was peaceful. Tired as I was, I didn't want to check in to my accommodation yet, as I'd probably lie on the bed and not get up again, and anyway, sore feet or not, it was a beautiful evening. The sunshine and tranquil atmosphere made me decide to set out for a walk around the town.

Diksmuide is compact, and I didn't have to walk far from the central square before I found myself alongside the still waters of a canal, next to which a group of teenagers moved excitedly around a jetty, manoeuvring an ingenious pontoon raft made from plastic barrels for launch. I passed the Béguinage, once home to the lay Christian order of the Beguines, who lived in voluntary poverty and tended the sick. There is a local story that Thomas Becket stayed here after being forced into exile by Henry II in 1164. He set out on a boat from Sandwich with two canons and a servant, arrived on the Flanders coast and spent the next six years mainly at Pontigny in the south of France, apparently passing through Diksmuide en route and finding lodging at the Béguinage, presenting the order with a chalice to mark his gratitude.

I made my way back past the strangely enormous St
Nicholas Church to the Grote Markt and the De Vrede
hotel, where I was to spend the night. I was led through a
courtyard at the back to a brand new building of light, airy
and modern rooms, all white walls, pine furniture, chrome
fittings and large windows that seemed at odds somehow
with the square I'd left behind a few yards away. The place
even smelled brand new. Over the bed, however, the only
interruption to the white, the pine and the chrome was a
large black-and-white print of a First World War trench.
Even here, in the town's newest and most modern establishment, the most apocalyptic event in Diksmuide's history is
never far away, and certainly never hidden.

13

'IT USED TO MAKE ME CRY SOMETIMES TO SEE A BIG MAN LIKE THAT GROVELLING FOR A LITTLE BIT OF BREAD'

The 10th Battalion of the Queen's (Royal West Surrey) Regiment was a product of the First World War. In February 1915, Lord Kitchener had approached the mayors of all twenty-eight London boroughs, emphasising the urgent need for recruits. This led in the spring of that year to the Great Metropolitan Recruiting Campaign, in which each mayor vowed to raise a local battalion drawn from the borough.

Battersea had provided men for an entire unit already in the trenches, the 23rd (County of London) Battalion, London Regiment, and the mayor was doubtful he could raise another significant body of men, but when his counterpart in Wandsworth made it known that he would be supplying 1,000 new recruits to the East Surrey Regiment as part of the project, it ignited a territorial political rivalry and a plan was launched for Battersea to bolster the ranks of the West Surreys to an equivalent or preferably higher number.

Battersea should have been a ripe recruiting ground. Like neighbouring Wandsworth, it was a poor borough: some 30 per cent of the residents of both boroughs lived below the poverty line, and in Battersea only one in ten boys stayed at school past the age of fourteen. Enlistment, with its regular wage, uniform and the promise of regular meals, was an attractive option. Well, as long as one overlooked the high probability of being killed, that is. Officials were confident of raising 1,350 men, of whom 1,100 would be battle ready as soon as possible, with the remainder staying in Battersea to staff the depot.

The Queen's, a venerable regiment that dates back to the days of Charles II, granted the Battersea battalion official status in June 1915, under the unwieldy official title of the 10th (Service) Battalion (Battersea), the Queen's (Royal West Surrey) Regiment. Later that month, the Old Etonian Colonel William Inglis was appointed commanding officer, despite not having seen military action since India the previous century. He was nevertheless hailed in the local press as 'a splendid commander, a thorough soldier and a thorough gentleman'. His adjutant was a 45-year-old Scot Lieutenant Alexander Lawrence, who'd served in France the previous year before being badly wounded.

Immediately, three councillors presented themselves at the town hall (now the Battersea Arts Centre) to enlist, but in the first week fewer than fifty local men followed them through the doors. Most of the Battersea men had, of course, already joined up, while the Royal Irish Rifles were already leading a successful campaign to recruit local men of Irish descent. The sight of wounded men being loaded into the local Bolingbroke Hospital wasn't ideal recruiting PR either. Not even the distribution by local women of spoof one-way rail tickets to Berlin among men of military age seemed to have much of an effect, and by the end of July the Battersea Battalion was only 100 strong, compared to the 700 who'd joined up over the boundary in Wandsworth. When a former Battersea councillor managed to badly injure himself during bomb-throwing practice on Clapham Common in October, it seemed as though the Battersea project might even be doomed.

However, the imminent passing of the Conscription Act in January 1916 brought a sudden rush of recruits, who realised that if they waited for the call they'd have no choice in the regiment to which they'd be posted. Suddenly, almost out of nowhere and almost by chance, the target was reached, and the battalion moved to the Albuhera Barracks in Aldershot. The 10th Queen's were in business.

It was 5 May 1916 when the battalion left for France – sailing from Southampton to Le Havre – arriving at six the following morning and immediately being posted to Outtersteene, west of Bailleul, on the French side of the border with Belgium. It wasn't long before the battalion was moved again, across the border to Ploegstraat, known to the Tommies as Plug Street, and into the line for the first time.

War for the 10th Queen's, as it was for most battalions, was a combination of heavy fighting and quieter periods out of the line spent training, drilling and resting. In June 1917 the 10th Queen's, including Victor Fagence, took part in the Battle of Messines, losing only seven men (with fourteen missing) from their battle strength of 626. The Third Battle of Ypres, however, saw the West Surreys suffer heavy casualties, exacerbated by further losses at the Battle of the Menin Road in September. These actions saw the end of George Fortune's involvement with the 10th Queen's and, indeed, his combat involvement in the war altogether.

As he recalled: 'When we arrived in Ypres, we lined up in the main square in front of the Cloth Hall, which was in ruins, and as the shells burst we ducked. Our CO rode up on his horse. He shouted, "You get used to this!", but at the same time he was ducking his old head too.'

When the battle commenced, even George, who took most things in his stride, was appalled by the conditions.

'There were no trenches,' he remembered. 'It was just mud; mud as far as you could see – they called it the Haig Ocean. We only did forty-eight hours in the line: we used to get so exhausted sinking in the mud, a lot of the chaps even used to drown in it. It meant our feet were always wet, and we had to try and dry our socks however we could: we used to wring them out and put them under our armpits in an effort to dry them. Of course, there were no latrines either. We used to go in empty bully tins during the days or hang on till the night: sometimes we'd go out over the top at night just to be able to move around and get warm.'

As the result of an unspecified misdemeanour, George was given a Field Punishment Number Two, in which he was detailed to carry the wounded from the battlefield to the dressing station. It was dangerous work in terrible conditions: 'It was always raining up there – you could only move slowly, especially in the dark. We would go a few yards, a

Verey light would go up and we would stand dead still because if you moved Jerry would see you. You'd wait until it went out, then you wouldn't see anything at all for a while, then off you'd go again, slipping and sliding. You didn't know where you were. The bloke we had was a German. We would slip and he'd fall off the stretcher and have to scramble back on again. Eventually we could see a big heap of mud above the ground that looked like a dugout. There were shell holes full of water between us and it, and we could not get near, so we put the stretcher down and went to look. There were men lying about all over the place asking us to help them. It was as much as we could do to keep afloat ourselves. Then we couldn't find our stretcher case again so we made our way back.'

Back in the trenches, George found that his water bottle had been holed and was empty, meaning he couldn't contribute any water to the tea. Knowing that his colleagues would insist he still had a share – fresh water was scarce at the front line – George pretended that he just didn't want any. An officer guessed the truth.

'He said, "You must" and "See me when you come out of the line",' George recalled. 'I went to see him, and he gave me another water bottle to sling around my neck and said, "Fortune, get your hair cut." Then he paused, and in a kind way he said, "It won't always be like this, Fortune." I heard he got killed shortly afterwards.'

Before the Battle of the Menin Road, the truth about George's age had come out. He was withdrawn from the line and sent back through the lines to Étaples. He went reluctantly, and alone.

'On I went walking and walking until I was halted by an artillery man,' he said. 'I asked him if he knew where Claridges Street was – that was the name of the place where I needed to go – but he seemed upset, and it turned out his mate had just been killed and was lying there, dead, by the gun. He said he had been with him all through the war. I told him I was going out because of my age. He said, "Good luck, mate," and gave me a good swig of rum. I don't know where he'd got it from but he had it in a petrol tin.'

The walk was difficult enough in the muddy conditions, but, like most of the men in the trenches, George's feet were in a bad way: 'Our feet were swollen. They brought us whale oil to rub into them – it was like engine oil. Our feet were rounded at the bottoms and we couldn't stand up properly. We laughed about it but it wasn't funny really.'

When he reached Étaples, rather than being sent home, George was kept there with other underage boys as part of a young soldiers' battalion. They'd train and drill until they were deemed old enough to go back into the lines. In the meantime, he was reintroduced to a morbidly familiar duty.

'I was back on the old burial fatigue,' said George. 'It was a sad business: the coffins were roughly made and sometimes the blood would come through the bottom. We all said we were going to be undertakers when we got home.'

George turned eighteen and went before the medical board. They gave him a B2 rating because of the varicose veins he'd developed from tying his puttees too tight. Instead of rejoining the 10th Queen's, George was instead sent to Gommecourt prisoner-of-war (POW) camp on the Somme, where the prisoners were given the dangerous task of being sent out to collect salvage from old battlefields.

'I got on well with the German prisoners; they were very like our own chaps,' said George. 'One of them was very like my dad, and I got on pretty well with him and would give him little bits of bread. He used to make paper knives out of the copper bands from the dud shells. He would come to the wire of the compound and call "sentry". I'd go over and he'd give me something he had made. It used to make me cry sometimes to see a big man like that grovelling for a little bit of bread.'

When he'd been at Gommecourt for a while, George was granted leave, the first time he'd been home in two years. He was told to report to Boulogne for delousing, but in his haste to see his mother again he dodged the disinfectant and hopped onto an earlier boat. He took the train from Folkestone to Victoria, picked up his £2 Prince of Wales relief fund at the station and went home to Highgate.

'Mother put all my clothes in the copper and I got into my civvies, which were too small for me by then,' he said. 'I didn't go out much, because it was just lovely to be in a house again.'

Leave was over all too quickly, and before he knew it George was on a boat back to Boulogne, where something remarkable occurred: 'While waiting to disembark I could hear someone on the quayside shouting, "Fortune! Fortune!" When I landed the voice was still calling. I went towards it and it was my brother Walter! I hugged and kissed him: I felt like a child again. He pushed me away and said, "Be your age, for Christ's sake!" He had been badly wounded in the leg and was now working in a field butchery in the docks, humping meat in the ice holds of ships. He told me the war would not last much longer. We said goodbye and off I went. He'd had a letter from Mother to say I was home on leave and had been meeting every ship coming in, calling out, "Fortune!" in the hope of seeing me.'

George saw out the war at the POW camp, and when he was demobbed returned to London on the same day as Walter. This is where we leave George Fortune, the young lad who watched Blériot land, stole a cap from a dead man and marched off to war. He went back to working on the London Underground, married and had two children, and died in 1978 at the age of 79. Things worked out for Walter, too, despite initial problems finding work. He'd report to Camden Labour Exchange every day and would talk to the girl who operated the lift at Camden Town Underground station about his predicament.

'One day she said to him, "I will get you a job,"' said George. 'She asked the station manager for time off and took him to the superintendent's office. She said she wanted him to have her job, and she carried on about him having fought for us. They gave my brother a different job, she kept hers, he married her and they eventually moved to New Zealand.'

Back at the Front, after their heavy losses in the autumn of 1917 the 10th Queen's regrouped at De Panne on the North Sea coast, where I began my walk across Flanders, and from there the Queen's were suddenly called away to Italy, a long and uncomfortable journey undertaken by, among others, Fred Dixon.

'We'd been holding the left flank of the whole of the western front,' he recalled, 'right up to the beach at Nieuwpoort in Belgium, the very end of the line. A friend of mine, Sgt Humphries, was in charge of part of a detachment which actually ran down the beach. He said he felt very aware that he was the very last in a line that stretched right down to Switzerland. We were in trenches on the banks of the canal and went back to a place called Guevelle, near Dunkirk, where we heard that four divisions were being sent to Italy, including ours. We were kitted out with replacements to clothes and equipment, and our boots received special attention: I even received a new pair.'

On 12 November, the 10th Queen's boarded a train near the Belgian border and embarked on an arduous journey to Mantua that would take a week. The carriages were filled to capacity, forty men in each, making lying down to sleep an impressive feat of recumbent choreography. The food was supplied by the battalion cooks, who travelled on open trucks with their equipment, but every meal had an obvious and tricky consequence for men tightly packed into carriages designed for cattle.

'It's obvious that at certain periods you had to stop to answer calls of nature,' said Fred. 'These calls can't be regulated by a railway timetable, so when these occasions did arise outside the train schedule then one had to either make a rush for the buffers or wait for the next stop. During the day the sliding doors were open and the troops stood or sat with their legs hanging out of the truck, but at night the doors were closed and they stayed that way until morning. But, of course, one's bladder didn't know that so we had to make arrangements. There was a small flap for ventilation at the top of each door, which for our purposes would have been far better placed about three feet from the floor. Anyone wanting to spend a penny had to negotiate the tight, packed, prostrate forms, as well as the jolting and rolling of the train. He next had to place a foot on a diagonal timber on the door, then, by means of the bars in the opening, he produced what I'd call the greatest acrobatic trick of all time.

'The people in the south of France actually seemed pleased to see us. At Nice we were bombarded with flowers as we passed slowly through the station; at Genoa we were treated to some wine; and on the platform at Alessandria, black coffee was distributed by civilians, which we all thought would have been nicer with a drop of milk. In our truck there was a peacetime tramp, a proper gentleman of the road by the name of Harper, and he said, "Don't drink the coffee until I get back," and left the truck. Three minutes later he arrived back with three tins of milk that he'd "found" in the quartermaster's truck. Useful chap to have around, was Harper.'

At the end of the rail journey, the 10th Queen's faced a march of some 120 miles to the banks of the River Piavé, in the north-east of Italy. It was a demanding distance on foot at the best of times, but the men were carrying their equipment, and more.

As Fred recalled: 'We were carrying full packs with two extra bandoliers of .303 ammunition and an egg bomb in each pocket as we didn't know who or what we might meet on the way, so we were pretty heavily laden. The blankets were stowed on the transport, meaning that every night you had a different one – it was hard to keep your strain of lice pure, that way. You could feel these things walking about the blanket, and I remember one night I had one that was so riddled I threw it off and did without it. The next morning it had gone, so someone had got a whole pack of trouble there.'

The march took ten days, including a couple of rest days. It was a remarkable feat, given the weight of the equipment and the fact that the men had been cooped up on a train for a week with no opportunity for exercise other than jumping down from the trucks and scampering for the bushes whenever the train stopped long enough for the call of nature to be answered. It was even more difficult if you were marching in brand new boots that had yet to be broken in.

'I soon had raw patches on my heels the size of half-crown pieces,' said Fred, 'and I'd pack handkerchiefs down the back of my boots because of the sores. Many of us were in the same state. It was hard going, all right. I remember one man, Corporal Mitchell, who in peace time was the manager of Clark's music shop in Basingstoke. He fell down beside me, unconscious. As I bent down the RSM roared at me to leave him alone; I just had time to grab his rifle and we marched on. Four hours later he arrived in the billet having walked all the way by himself.

'Food was in short supply, and that's the thing all my pals remembered about that Italian march. Rations were very meagre; the grapevine said they'd been diverted to Switzerland by mistake, so we used to visit farmhouses to obtain polenta and milk, but our financial resources were so small we were glad that our money was never accepted. These were poor people who could ill afford it, but we never had to pay for anything.'

On reaching the Piavé, the battalion was required to cover the eastern end of the Montelo hill and prevent incursions by the Austrians. Fred was by this stage an accomplished signaller and the man the officers went to when it came to communications: 'A friend and I were detailed to set up a station to link to a battery of 18-pounder guns, capable of sending an SOS by power buzzer to the little village where the battery was located, telling them they could get into action and where they should aim. The station had to be manned every minute of the twenty-four hours and it was usually me up there with another chap, and we sat in one of those big farmhouse fireplaces where you looked up the chimney and saw the sky. The occupiers had fled, leaving all their possessions. There were only two of us, so the one who was off-duty had to do all the cooking and everything for the chap who was on. Rations were brought up to us each day and we were there for a fortnight doing six hours on, six off, and with all the other things you had to do there wasn't a lot of time left for sleeping. In the first week it snowed, and the gunners put a lone gun in a barn across the road. I don't know why. We were way out in front of the battery, but an Austrian aeroplane had seen the tracks of the gun in the snow and they put their 5.9s on it, one of which came through the wall of the farmhouse and into the next room.

'The farmer returned with his wife the following week, and when she went into the shelled room and saw the damage you've never heard anything like it. Her apron was over her head and she was howling her head off. She came back into the kitchen and I heard one of the gunners say, "For Christ's sake, put that laughing record on." It was some kind of music hall thing on which the singer was killing himself laughing, and it's a tribute to him that in a few seconds her howling had stopped, her apron came off her head and she began to smile. She couldn't locate where the sound was coming from – she thought I had something to do with it in the fireplace – but she was shrieking with laughter and slapping her thighs in merriment.'

In March 1918 the 10th Queen's were sent back to the Western Front, just in time to catch the full onslaught of the German Spring Offensive at the Somme. Following the October Revolution of 1917, the Russians had left the war, meaning all the German units that had been fighting on the eastern front could now be deployed to the west. An extraordinary onslaught, the biggest of the war, started on 21 March, beginning with artillery and gas barrages and followed by the massed infantry. On that day alone, the Germans gained four miles and accounted for more than 30,000 Allied lives. By early April they had pushed so far west that their long-range guns could reach Paris. They were very close to winning the war.

Like most regiments, the 10th Queen's suffered great losses. Of the 902 men who faced the Germans, only 379 survived. William Dann was one of them: 'Our part of the line was in a horseshoe, with Germans on each side as well as in front. The next morning the Germans attacked and we managed to beat them off, helped by the double row of barbed wire in front of us. That evening they attacked again and we knocked them off again. The next morning at daybreak they attacked for a third time. We were holding him quite well and we'd say to one another, he'll never get through here, we'll be all right. Then over to our right we could see men running down the hill: the Germans had broken through there instead. Eventually an officer came along and said, "They're through and it's every man for himself," so we packed up the gun and headed back. The Germans were putting up a terrific barrage and coming through the barbed wire at us. We had small fire, hand grenades at the back of us and a barrage in front of us. It was very disorganised and we didn't know who was who, what was what or where was where. Eventually we got back to our horse lines where there were troughs, and I remember taking my tin hat off and drinking the water out of this horse trough.

'For ten days we didn't really know what was going on and were dawdling about in different directions, hoping we were going towards where our people were, but it took that full ten days before we could stop and get organised again. Eventually we sorted ourselves out and everyone rejoined their units, although there weren't many of us left.'

The shocked survivors from the West Surreys were marched to Poperinge and rested for two days, which is, I think, where Edward Connelly's war actually began. It was also where I was heading myself.

14

'I AM TROUBLED WITH MY HEAD AND CANNOT STAND THE SOUND OF THE GUNS'

From Diksmuide I set out early for Poperinge along the Ijser canal, which effectively had been the Belgian front line for almost the entire war.

I paused at the IJzertoren, which I'd previously seen from the horizon. First erected by an organisation of Flemish soldiers in 1920 to remember their fallen comrades, the original tower was blown up one night in March 1946. The perpetrators were never caught and nobody claimed responsibility, but it's believed to have been the work of anti-Flemish French nationalists, possibly in response to alleged collaboration with the Nazis by some Flemish speakers in the region.

Either way, the rebuilt town across the canal should have made it clear to the bombers that, if they tore down the tower, it would only go straight back up again. A new one was erected, exactly the same as the original, only seventy feet taller. At the top of the tower, as with the original, are the letters AVV–VVK, standing for *Alles voor Vlaanderen, Vlaanderen voor Kristus* ('All for Flanders, Flanders for Christ') in an acrostic, which enshrined the tower as both a memorial and a rallying point for Flemish nationalists and separatists. The fact that the tower was built to look like the Flemish-designed gravestones originally given to the Flemish fallen of the war, which also carried the slogan, caused French-speaking Belgians to raise a quizzical eyebrow (indeed, the official removal and destruction of the headstones to be replaced by a uniform one for all the Belgian dead was part of the motivation for the tower in the first place).

Today, however, it's as a peace memorial that the tower stands, containing a rather good museum of the First World War ranging up the twenty-two storeys of its interior. At the roadside, a rubble stone arch – made from what remained of the original tower – inlaid with the word 'pax' serves as the entrance. This combination of peace symbol and focus for the national-identity crisis strikes me as very Belgian, but I found the tower a little too forbidding for my palate; it's awesome in the same way as an old power station, its dark brickwork and thumping in-your-face design something quite different from the symbolism of the restored Grote Markt.

Once I'd passed the tower, the walk alongside the Yser was enough to lift anyone's spirits. It was a cool, sunny morning, the water was mirror still and the birds were singing in the trees. Apart from the occasional passing cyclist and the odd fisherman sitting on the bank, I appeared to have the countryside all to myself. A distant church steeple was the only human structure that punctured the horizon for as far as I could see. It was impossible to imagine this tranquil route as an artery of relentless horror for the entire duration of the war.

I stopped for a rest at a picnic table close to a bridge over the canal and spread out my map to check on my progress. After a couple of minutes, a black SUV with dark windows came to a halt nearby, the low thump of music from inside disappearing as the engine was killed. The door opened and a balding man in his thirties jumped down, in T-shirt, jeans and mirrored aviator sunglasses. He greeted me in Dutch, soon twigged that I was English and a stilted conversation followed: my Dutch is non-existent; he was reaching back to long-forgotten schoolboy English lessons. He'd come to fish. He'd be here all day and stay here all night, too. He indicated the tent bag over his shoulder and nodded vigorously, his smile suggesting that he'd been looking forward to this nocturnal expedition for quite some time.

'You like Belgium?' he asked. I confirmed that, yes, I like Belgium, very much. 'Belgium is cool, huh?' he added. I agreed, even though such an endorsement from a sweaty, whiskery man in walking gear might not carry much weight in the higher echelons of cool.

'Not Brussels, though,' he went on, frowning. 'Brussels is not cool.'

I asked why. He made a face and waved a hand to indicate that his English wasn't up to an explanation, then asked what I was doing. Walking, I said: walking across Flanders from London.

'Ah,' he said, 'that is my dream …' before tailing off and looking away to the horizon. If it was the freedom of the road for which he hankered, considering he would spend the next twenty-four hours by the side of an idyllic rural waterway waiting for the fish to bite, he really wasn't doing too badly himself. Whatever Brussels-related trauma he may have suffered, this looked like the perfect antidote.

A couple of miles further on a car slowed alongside me, probably the first car to pass me all morning. A grey-haired man with extraordinarily good teeth smiled at me from the driver's seat. From between the two immaculate pearly rows came a stream of Flemish. I smiled weakly and apologised for not understanding a word. He switched immediately into perfect English and offered me a lift. He seemed stunned at my polite decline but the smile never wavered. 'Are you sure?' he asked. I was quite sure, thank you, but he was very kind. 'Really?' he said with a tangible note of surprise. Yes, really, thank you, I prefer to walk.

The smile flickered with incomprehension for an instant, but he nodded at me and drove off, waving. I wonder what he was smiling about. It might just have been trapped wind.

I left the Yser and headed south-west, reaching the tiny village of Reninge just as the church bells were battering the living daylights out of midday. It was hot and dusty as I passed on through Oostvleteren. My feet were sore from the relentless tarmac pounding, and by the time I made it to Poperinge in the early evening I was almost ready to drop. I parked myself on a bench in the Grote Markt to the accompanying tinkle of cutlery, as waiters in white aprons laid the outdoor tables of the restaurants. A gaggle of laughing teenagers crossed the square, and two local women greeted each other with smiles and kisses a few feet from where I was sitting. Such an atmosphere of bonhomie was entirely appropriate because, unlike many – or indeed most – of the

Western Front towns, Poperinge's connection to the war is an overwhelmingly positive one.

Poperinge lies eight miles west of Ypres and, save for a fleeting German occupation in the early days of the war, remained behind the Allied lines for the entire conflict. Its proximity to the Front, behind Ypres, made Poperinge an important gateway, and countless thousands of British soldiers would have passed through on their way to and from the Front, Edward included.

Although it suffered occasional shelling from long-range German artillery, 'Pops', as the town became known to the British troops, was a haven, a respite, a welcome sight and about the closest they'd get to normality after leaving England. During the war, the square where I sat was lined with cafés and souvenir shops, while impromptu stalls and dealers exercised a roaring trade in black market goods, to which the British military hierarchy turned a blind eye. Here, soldiers away from the Front could relax, sit in cafés with a pot of tea, eat egg and chips and buy souvenirs and postcards to send home. Poperinge was as close to a happy place as anywhere on the Western Front could be for the British soldier abroad, and my initial impression was that it's a feeling that prevails today.

The relative lack of damage suffered by the town meant that, unusually for this area, most of the buildings on the square pre-date the war, although only just in the case of the imposing 1911 neo-gothic town hall, away to my right.

One that didn't, behind me to my left, was a café called La Poupée ('The Doll'). This one is a modern building now, but its namesake predecessor was one of Poperinge's, and by extension the Western Front's, most famous establishments.

When war broke out and arrived on the doorstep, Elie Crossey realised that his shoemaker's and his wife's haberdashery businesses were immediately under threat. People would have more pressing things to spend money on than new shoes and lacy drawers, assuming they were going to stick around dodging the shells in the first place. Fortunately, Elie had a keen eye for the main chance and, spying the hundreds of troops arriving in the town, soon converted their premises on the Grote Markt (or Grand Place as it was then) into a café called La Poupée. There were a number of cafés in Poperinge administering to the thirsts and needs of British troops milling around the town at any one time – Cyrill's, the Four Crowns, the What 'Opes, not to mention the famous Talbot House – so Elie decided to make his establishment not just any old café, but one to which only officers could gain admittance.

One contemporary visitor described La Poupée as a 'cheery spot' with clean tablecloths and flowers in pots on the tables, about as far from tins of bully beef and mess dishes of weak stew in a muddy trench as could be imagined. It must have been an extraordinary feeling for men accustomed to the mud and rations of the trenches, wolfed down from a battered mess tin with dirty cutlery held in filth-encrusted hands wherever you stood, to travel just a few miles and be served tea as if you were in an English market town on a holiday weekend, yet still be just a few miles from the most dangerous place in the world.

What set La Poupée apart from the rest of the cafés was neither the décor nor the board of fare. The Crosseys' three flame-haired daughters were the key to the establishment's success, and in particular the youngest, Eliane, nicknamed 'Ginger', who would come to be so popular with visiting officers that the café became better known among the officers as 'Ginger's'. Eliane was barely a teenager when war broke out, but her striking red hair and effervescent personality made her a legend of the front line: officers on leave would make straight for the café in the hope of seeing Ginger and, if they were lucky, being given one of the signed photographs she saved for a chosen few.

These days there is something a little icky about grown men going starry-eyed over a girl who would only turn 16 two weeks after the armistice, but Ginger would have been a light of innocence among the hellish surroundings. Ginger's popularity stemmed from her inherent goodness and sunny nature, which charmed the officers; maybe she reminded them of younger sisters, goddaughters or nieces and happier, more innocent times. Whatever it was, throughout the war there are constant references in diaries and letters to the magnificence of Ginger of Poperinge.

Eliane stayed on after the war as the café became a boarding house for people travelling to see the battlefields, but there is some uncertainty as to her eventual fate. Most accounts say that she married a businessman from Bruges and relocated to England, only to perish in an air raid in 1942, aged forty, but there doesn't seem to be an official record of her death in England. She certainly travelled to England at one stage soon after the war, as she was invited to a remembrance event at the Albert Hall and was received at Buckingham Palace, such was the affection with which she was remembered by the men who passed through La Poupée.

Once the throbbing in the soles of my feet had died down
a little, I stood up, hauled my rucksack onto my shoulder
and crossed to the Hotel de la Paix in the corner of the
Grote Markt, where I was given a room on the first floor
with a terrific view across the square. As night fell I sat in
the hotel restaurant with a Poperings Hommel Bier
(Poperinge is at the heart of hop country; 80 per cent of the
nation's hops are grown in the area) and, looking out as
night fell, it was easy to imagine Poperinge coming to life a
century earlier, lights coming on in the bars and restaurants,
the sound of boots on the cobbles, the occasional clatter of
horses' hoofs, a sudden burst of laughter and music as a café
door opens and closes, the orange pinpricks of countless
cigarettes in the dark and an overwhelming feeling of bois-
terous relief.

The next morning I explored the other, darker side of
Poperinge's wartime legacy. In the courtyard of the town hall
stands a pole. As killing grounds go, this is an incongruous
one in a region more versed in death than most, but the pole
represents the place where at least four British soldiers were
executed by their own side. It's not the original one – there's
some debate as to whether it's even vaguely in the right
place – but it's an evocative reminder of one of the war's
grubbier aspects. A door in the archway leading to the
courtyard takes you to the 'death cells', two tiny rooms
where the convicted men would, it's claimed, have spent
their last hours. In one, the walls are protected by Perspex
sheets, behind which are preserved countless examples of
Great War graffiti: these weren't just execution cells –
soldiers found drunk, who were out beyond the terms of

their passes, found in bars and cafés when they shouldn't have been, or had committed similar misdemeanours, would spend the night here. There are names, dates, regimental badges and the odd obscene cartoon carved into the plaster of walls, exercises in passing time that left a permanent representation of a soldier's presence here. The other cell is locked but an aperture in the door allows you to see inside the darkened room, where a film on a constant loop recreates a soldier spending his last night before execution.

The most diverting aspect of the cells for me, however, was the accounts on the information boards of some of the men whom it's believed were executed here. The stories are heart-rending.

On 10 December 1916 at 7:25 a.m., for example, 2nd Lieutenant Eric Poole, aged thirty-one, of the 11th Battalion, West Yorkshire Regiment, was executed for desertion by firing squad. Born in Nova Scotia, Poole had served nearly three years in the Halifax Rifles there a decade prior to the war, before moving to Guildford with his family in 1905. He enlisted in 1914 and received an officer's commission the following year, but on 7 July 1916 Poole was wounded by an artillery shell at the Somme and left with as clear a case of shell shock as one could imagine. Despite this, barely two months later Poole was sent back to the Somme and, on 5 October, went missing as his unit advanced to the front line. Two days later he was arrested wandering aimlessly some four miles from where he had disappeared and charged with desertion. A medical assessment concluded that his mental state had contributed significantly to his absenting himself, but despite this and his recent treatment for shell shock,

Lieutenant-General Sir Henry Rawlinson insisted that Poole be court-martialled.

A medical report determined that Poole was 'of nervous temperament, useless in action and dangerous as an example to the men'. Another stated that, 'I am of the opinion that excitement may bring on a condition which would not make him responsible for his actions at that time.' His battalion quartermaster averred that Poole's mental disposition was more susceptible to shell shock than most.

Despite these clear opinions, the court martial found Poole to be 'of sound mind'. Of his desertion it was decided that he was 'capable of appreciating … such an act was wrong'. It conceded that he 'appeared dull under cross-examination and his perception is slow', but put that down to his 'mental powers [being] less than average'. Eric Poole was sentenced to death on 5 October, the sentence was confirmed by General Sir Douglas Haig the next day ('I see no extenuating circumstances and recommend that the sentence be carried out') and Poole was shot by firing squad four days later.

There's a photo of Eric Poole alongside his story. He's in civilian clothes – a high, stiff Edwardian collar with a tie and dark jacket – and flanked by his wife and daughter; it dates presumably from before the war, but while Mrs Poole regards the camera with half interest and the daughter looks straight down the lens, her mouth set in a determinedly tight-lipped line, Poole himself looks away, over the photographer's right shoulder. His gaze is distant and distracted, through heavy-lidded eyes, and his shoulders have a slight droop: he gives the impression of only being half present. One shouldn't read too much into a single photograph, but there's a tangible melancholy in Poole's demeanour, as well as a sense in his eyes that a part of him is missing, is elsewhere. With the benefit of knowing his story one can see how the quartermaster might conclude he was more susceptible to shell shock than 'ordinary' men.

Poole was very rare in being executed as an officer: only two other British officers were executed during the First World War, and he was the first. Of the ordinary ranks, one of the most poignant cases was that of Herbert Morris of the 2nd Battalion, British West Indies Regiment, who also appears on the wall at Poperinge. Just sixteen when he volunteered on his home island of Jamaica, Morris sailed across the Atlantic with his regiment to be thrown immediately into the preparations for the Third Battle of Ypres in the summer of 1917. The British West Indies Regiment was not a combat regiment, but it was assigned to assist a battery of giant 80-pounder guns at Essex Farm, not far from Poperinge, in laying down an intense barrage ahead of the infantry charge. A Flemish priest recalled how the West Indian lads became 'enormously afraid of the guns'. Morris went AWOL, was picked up at Boulogne attempting to cross to England and given fourteen days' field punishment. On 20 August 1917 Morris disappeared again, jumping from the lorry in which he was travelling to a work party, and he was again arrested at Boulogne. He complained, 'I am troubled with my head and cannot stand the sound of the guns.' Morris, who had by now turned seventeen, received two positive character reports but was found guilty and shot in the early morning of 20 September 1917. The firing squad of ten included seven soldiers from the West Indies.

Three hundred and forty-six soldiers of the British Army were executed during the First World War, a little over 10 per cent of the 3,080 who received the death sentence. The majority were charged with desertion, many with cowardice, a few with casting away their arms and a handful with murder. Most had their sentences commuted to a term in prison, suspended so that they could return to the line rather than see out the war in a cell, but given the cases of Eric Poole and Herbert Morris one wonders what it was about their particular situations that led to their execution when most of those charged with similar offences were spared the blindfold and cigarette. The need to make an example, perhaps – to maintain discipline. We are a lot more aware of mental health issues today, but even so, Poole's case in particular seems to be a terrible miscarriage.

Despite the dark presence of the death cells so close to its heart, Poperinge still retained its cheery air as I crossed the Grote Markt. The weekly market was in full swing and I was assailed with smells and sights as I moved away from the grim legacy of the execution post. The combined aroma of cheese, fish and freshly baked cakes and pastries has lingered over this spot since Poperinge's early medieval origins (Sir Thopas, Chaucer's knight from *The Canterbury Tales*, was from Poperinge) but it was another piece of First World War history for which I was heading.

If Poperinge's cafés and establishments returned a little dimly remembered humanity to the lives of many British soldiers during the war, then Talbot House brought an entirely new level of civilisation. Talbot House was the brainchild of a young vicar named Philip Clayton, best known by his childhood nickname of Tubby (he'd been a school contemporary of G.K. Chesterton and is thought to have been the inspiration for his clerical detective, Father Brown). Clayton arrived in Poperinge in 1915 as an army chaplain and soon determined that he could minister to the soldiers' spiritual needs in ways far beyond the simply religious.

When he had the opportunity to install himself in a château a couple of minutes' walk from the Grote Markt in Poperinge, vacated by its owner once hostilities heated up, Tubby Clayton set about creating what would become one of the most extraordinary stories of the First World War. With a colleague, Neville Talbot, he had the slight artillery damage to the building repaired, named the place Talbot House after Neville's brother, who had been killed a few months earlier, opened it as 'Every Man's Club' and the legend of Toc H (from the signallers' code for Talbot House) was born.

Inside the house, soldiers could drink tea in the conservatory or the garden, peruse the house's remarkably well-stocked library, gather round the piano for a sing-song or attend (and even participate in) the regular revues, soirées and concerts that took place there. It was a tremendous piece of home far from home.

Today, Talbot House has been preserved almost exactly as Tubby Clayton left it and how the thousands of soldiers who passed through would have remembered it. There's a museum attached that tells the story and displays some of the objects associated with it, but the true spirit of the place is in the house itself. Having passed through the museum and walked across the well-tended lawn into the conservatory, I was immediately offered a cup of tea by a friendly

Scotsman called George, one of the volunteers who staff the house. He asked if I was with one of the coach parties and, when I said I was a lone traveller, conspiratorially told me I could have a mug rather than a small cup. I liked George. I sat at a table in the conservatory with my mug and watched the coach parties troop in, all of them equally delighted by the offer of tea from George and his teenage daughter.

I climbed the stairs to the first floor and peered into what had been Tubby's bedroom-cum-office, the sign on the door declaring his philosophy: 'All rank abandon ye who enter here.' Brigadier or private, everyone was equally welcome and treated in exactly the same way at Talbot House. One floor up was the room used as a theatre and concert hall, where a film played of a reconstruction of a concert, at which, as recorded in Clayton's memoirs, an unknown officer stood up on stage one night and beautifully performed a music-hall song wrung through with the emotion of loss before disappearing into the night never to be seen again.

On the top floor, up in the eaves and accessed by a steep, narrow set of steps that are more ladder than staircase, is the chapel, its altar constructed from an old saw horse, where Clayton would conduct his services. Even for someone of no religion, it was a moving place to stand and think about the thousands of young men – who knows, maybe even Edward himself – who had climbed those stairs and prayed before heading to the Front, from where many of them would never return.

Despite being a converted attic with a saw horse for an altar, there is an atmosphere of piety and reverence to match that of the largest and oldest vaulted-roof English church. It retains a very real sense of the hopes and dreams of the frightened men who passed through.

It is extraordinary how a building with a special past can retain a specific atmosphere. It should just be bricks and mortar, but the house is infused with a benevolence and calmness that surely stems from the days of Tubby Clayton and the happy house he ran here. Even for the coach parties, a cup of tea in the conservatory provides a welcome taste of home, so one can only imagine what it must have been like for a man just back from the Front, the shelling still ringing in his ears and the lice tickling his collar, and it's a feeling that prevails today. As authentic First World War experiences go, Talbot House may not have the crash, bang, wallop and mud and hell of the trenches, but as far as taking you back to the second decade of the twentieth century goes, it really can't be beaten.

Reluctantly, I left the welcoming calm of Talbot House and set out for Ypres. This was my shortest walking day; there are roughly eight miles between Poperinge and Ypres, but this was the first time I felt I was truly walking in Edward's footsteps. It was 'only' eight miles, but it was a march that took the men from the relative safety and welcoming embrace of Tubby Clayton and Ginger Crossey into the reality of the war. The road to Ypres passed along a landscape pulped by the legacy of conflict and, as Ypres drew nearer, the soldiers would find themselves in a land of flooded shell holes, shattered tree stumps and the constant presence of death.

15

'WE USED TO SIT IN THE CORNER OF THE TRENCH AND THINK ABOUT IT: WE'D SAY, ALL THIS GOING ON, IS IT WORTH IT?'

When Edward arrived at Poperinge in early April 1918 what sort of conditions would he have found? The war had been raging for almost four years by that stage so the Western Front would have presented a landscape of uninterrupted mass destruction. Trenches would have snaked through the shell-battered battlefield, barely a tree would have stood higher than a blasted stump and most of the towns and villages would have been flattened or, at best, badly damaged. He would have arrived to join a battalion that was exhausted, in shock from the intensity of the German onslaught and trying to come to terms with losing nearly two thirds of their complement in the futile attempts to hold the Germans at bay. In April 1918 there was the very real sense that the Allies were on the point of losing the war. Morale wasn't exactly at its highest.

'That was the worst time,' said William Dann. 'You couldn't get it any worse, I should think, beyond earthquakes and volcanic eruptions. We used to sit in the corner of the trench and think about it; we'd say, all this going on, is it worth it? I used to think if I ever get out of this lot I shall be damned lucky. A lot of them were a little bit religious and you'd ask, "If there's a God about, why the hell doesn't he stop all this?" A lot of that went on amongst the men: why's it carrying on? What's it worth? Nobody really spoke up in favour of the war. You'd just go up and out, up and out, front line and back, front line and back, and got on with it. I never heard people discussing why the war started; we just knew we had to stick at it or stop there altogether.'

'Conditions were very bad,' according to Victor Fagence, now recovered from his wounds and back at the Front with a greater respect for his own mortality. 'All the shell holes filled with water and mud. You couldn't march over the mud. They made plank roads to a further distance, then duckboard tracks. It wasn't a very nice thing going up to the front line. All the way up you were liable to come under shell fire at any moment. The Germans knew the ground; it had been fought over for so long they knew the ranges of all the spots. They had their observation balloons and aircraft and knew exactly where the tracks were, and so you'd always come under shell fire. It was so bad that there were cases of men drowning in shell holes if they slipped off the duckboards with their packs on. When you reached the Front there were no trenches any more, just shell holes made into defences, about fifty yards apart. From there the German lines were a couple of hundred yards away, so they were very primitive living conditions. There were no latrines and you had to stay in these shell holes all day. You could only leave the trench at night and so had go to the toilet then. It was very uncomfortable.'

Stretcher-bearer Walter Cook was also in the area at the time and held a similar view of the conditions: 'Living conditions were always beyond description: the rain, the wet, the cold. You can't keep a uniform on for three weeks in those conditions. Lice abounded. A candle along the seams crackled them off, but there were no facilities for washing clothes. In Armentières there was a great big brewery and we bathed in the vats, the only bath I had in the whole war.

'In dugouts the rats were fearless, but some chaps had worse experiences – some had their ear nibbled, their ration biscuit eaten; wherever there was a grave or a body there were rats. In some of the trenches where men died, they were rolled into the cavity and there would be rats there; if they were buried in a field there'd be rats. The rats were deeply unpleasant animals because of their filtration into the graves.

'Ypres was terrible for gangrene: men had to stand for days in two or three feet of water. They were supposed to take their boots off and rub their feet with fat, but they'd come down to us and they'd be black. You sent them straight down the line to have their legs off. Hundreds of them.'

There was never a good time to arrive at the First World War, but it seems Edward turned up when things were about as bad as they could be. What was left of the 10th Queen's were utterly despondent and looking back on terrible losses – Fred Dixon said they were known at this time as the 'sacrifice battalion' – and this was on top of the knowledge that the Germans had made tremendous advances. At that stage prospects must have looked as bleak as they could be.

But trench life had to go on. There were still gas attacks to look out for, raids to carry out – and defend – and the rhythms of the war carried on as they always had.

'The trenches always had to be kept in repair,' said Charles Ward of that spring. 'If you had two or three days' rain, the earth would wash down the ramparts into the trench and you'd have to keep repairing it, that was normal work. Most of the time we were there to be prepared for anything happening. We didn't have any particular duties, we just kept ourselves tidy, our weapons clean and the trench in good condition. Other than that there wasn't much to do except chat among ourselves.'

Gas attacks were regular occurrences, and Edward would have kept his mask close at all times. Shells would normally announce themselves with a whistle or a whine but gas could arrive silently, creeping across the terrain, its tendrils working their way inside your lungs before you knew it. Old shell casings were hung up in the trenches and, in the event of a suspected gas attack, someone would bash the hell out of them with a stick to raise the alarm. Then would follow Wilfred Owen's 'ecstasy of fumbling' as the men fiddled with the straps and pulled their masks over their heads.

'As far as gas is concerned, you never knew,' said Charles Ward. 'For instance, you could be going along, leaving the front line to go to the rear, and at some time during the day the Germans would drop some gas down. They continually did that at Ypres – the gas shells were continually dropping, and one of our duties at night was to keep our eyes open for any gas. There was no guarantee that you could escape; it could just creep up on you. I went into hospital on one occasion and their first question was, "When were you gassed?" and I had to say I didn't realise I had been. On one occasion I remember taking a message to a camp where they'd had a gas attack, and it was only when I got there I discovered everyone wearing their gas masks, so maybe it was then.

'The lavatory was behind the line and no one went there during the day. When it got to dusk, that's when they'd go. On one occasion, this chap went to the latrine and the Germans knew he was there so they dropped over a few shells, including a gas one. He got very frightened and came rushing into our trench shouting, "Gas!" Two of us got hold of him, tied him down on our firing step, put his mask on, put our masks on and called a stretcher-bearer to take him away.'

Walter Cook, the stretcher-bearer who'd joined up after hearing his uncle's heart-breaking tales of men being left behind on the battlefield, was gassed so badly he had to go back to Britain, and he left one of the most vivid accounts of its effects.

'We were south of Épehy when I was gassed,' he said. 'The trenches were shallow and in my section there were four of us. We dug out the trenches to deepen them and were there for three days. The Germans started bombarding us with gas shells from around three in the afternoon to midnight. Eight hours in a gas mask – you had no feeling in your scalp at all after that. It was easy enough to breathe, though; I can't remember much difficulty if you used them the right way.

'The shelling stopped and it was a bit breezy and the gas seemed to clear. Then Jerry started with a high-explosive shell that hit the trench and part buried us, and while we struggled to get out we got the gas. We didn't notice it at the time – our turn of duty was done and we settled down for a doze, still in the front line.

'We woke up and my eyes were beginning to close, and that's when I realised we'd been gassed. My eyes were burning and I was bringing up a greenish foam. I'd lost my voice, too. With me was a Welshman called Davies, who was using the most frightful language I had ever heard, and another boy was crying for his mother: all of us had got the gas. There were about twelve of us altogether; we formed a crocodile and left the trenches for the casualty clearing station. We couldn't see – we were holding onto the shoulder of the man in front and the first man was being led by someone who could see. I was last in the crocodile. Our eyes were all gummed up and burning, and we were being sick with this green foam coming up from the lungs. After a time that stopped, but I still felt awful and was scared I'd lose my sight permanently. I don't know how far we went but it seemed to take quite a while. When we got there we were stripped of all our clothing and put in a tepid bath. My testicles were burning, too; mustard gas affects the moist areas of the body. It wasn't too bad, though; I think the bathing prevented it getting worse. Then we were given a suit of pyjamas and what they called a dolly bag, a cotton bag with a string to close it. Our uniform was put into it and it was hung from our wrists. I don't remember there being any treatment as such beyond the bath. It was a big marquee, a gigantic one, and there were quite a lot of us in it. We were given a hot drink but I couldn't taste anything – it could have been soup, coffee, cocoa or anything: as I couldn't see it didn't really matter.

'The next thing I remember is being in the general hospital at Rouen and being given a card to send home. I forced my eye open and could see a dazzling light, so I knew I still had my sight, but my voice had gone, I could barely whisper. Three or four times a day we were given a mask to breathe through for about an hour that had a musky sort of smell. I didn't like it. I presume it was some kind of chemical treatment but it was nauseating. After Rouen we were brought to Le Havre, from there to Southampton and I landed up in hospital in Whalley, near Blackburn. It was built as a lunatic asylum just before the war and was commandeered as a military hospital.

'I could see when I got there,' said Walter. 'Some friends of the family came to see me from Bolton to report back to the family, and I was able to see them once my eyes had opened properly. I couldn't open my eyes for four or five weeks and they were sensitive for years afterwards. They'd water even in a slight breeze. My lungs seemed fairly normal, beyond a bit of a cough.'

James Watson of the Northumberland Fusiliers was also gassed in Belgium: 'The billet we were in was a broken-down house, and we slept in the cellar during the day and went out digging trenches at night. The Germans sent it over in little shells that exploded next to where we were. I felt a bit groggy, and when daylight came and we had to go back to our billets, I started to be sick. And within half an hour, half of the men with me were dead. Most of them were burnt under the arms and between the legs. I was blind for a few days and was sent to a makeshift hospital in a lot of pain. The treatment they were giving us wasn't making any headway so they shifted us further back. They put some chemicals in my eyes and in some hot water, from a tin kettle. They put a blanket over my head and I had to inhale the steam from the spout of the kettle.'

When I read the accounts of men who were there around the time my great-uncle arrived, Edward slots straight in to the war narrative in my mind. He was trained, he was officially an infantryman, and he knew how to fire a gun and could presumably handle a bayonet. He knew his gas drill inside out. He'd have been drilled in trench digging and could by now march for England. But this was different. This wasn't training; this was the real thing. He might not have known a soul when he arrived and, given what the remaining members of the 10th had recently been through, backslapping welcomes and cheery bonhomie were probably not a feature of his arrival. I thought of his first night, wherever he might have been billeted, under a rough blanket somewhere, maybe in a bell tent with seventeen snoring, farting, burping strangers, all clawing away at themselves as the lice ran rampant through their clothes and blankets. Laying there in the dark he must have thought of home, of his mother, his grandparents, his baby goddaughter. For all the training, the barracks, the trains, the marching, all the alien things he'd done over the previous weeks, on that first night at the Front with his new comrades in arms home must never have seemed so far away.

Maybe he had a couple of letters stashed in his uniform, photographs maybe that he could look at to remind him of home. The distribution of letters was efficiently done throughout the war as the army realised how important it was for morale. Most of the correspondence sent to the trenches didn't survive – let's just mention the fact that the latrines were never supplied with toilet paper and leave it there – but in the Imperial War Museum archive I managed to find a thin, flimsy missive, the paper brown with age and as delicate as ancient papyrus, sent to William Dann by his father. It's dated 2 February 1918.

Dear Will,

Just a line to you in answer to your letter received quite safe. I was glad to hear from you and also that you received the cigarettes quite safe. I expect they are nearly all gone by now, we must send you some more now soon – that is if you are not getting leave yet. You had better answer this the first chance you get upon receiving it and let me know if possible when you get leave.

If you think there is time to send more out before you come I will send them out at once. But they seem to take seven or eight days before they get them to you and I should not like for them to arrive and you have left before they arrived.

But still, we could not help that, would much rather see you and lose them. But let me know if you can, then we will.

Ted and me are still at Newhaven on the transports. We are all settled and got used to the work now. We have shipped a lot of aircraft to Italy lately besides other things so expect they mean business.

I hope you are still having warm weather days out there and hope it is getting warmer nights for you. Are you still back from the line or have you been up again?

We are on rations now. One third each for meat, ¼lb margarine each and 2oz of tea a week each and the meat includes bacon so we shall not be overdone with it. But we get a meal every day at Newhaven so we shall not do too bad considering we shall have to buckle in our belts a bit.

Mabel and Ted are quite well and send their love to you. We are longing to see you again and hope it will not be too long.

Mabel's husband was home for a weekend last week but has gone out for a course of firing this week and will be gone about a month or so.

We are on nights this week. We do not get a lot of time to ourselves now but never mind, I expect you do not get any more so we must not grumble.

Hope to hear from you soon and good news at that on to when we see you again.

They have started women labour down at Newhaven now. There is a good many there, do not know whether they will stick it or not.

I think that is nearly all the news now and I must get to bed as we have to leave home at 9 o'clock tonight.

Take great care of yourself, old boy, and get your leave as soon as you can. Let me know when you get this about the smokes.

From your loving father.

Look after yourself all you can.

Sitting in an archive in South London on a rainy afternoon nearly a century after it was written, I was more moved by this letter than by anything else in all the soldiers' accounts I read while researching the kind of war Edward would have experienced. The cheery tone, the trivia, the practicalities of cigarette dispatch – it's the thinnest of veneers covering the most heart-breaking bottomless well of emotion.

It had been more than a year since William Dann's father had last seen him. William must have mentioned the possibility of coming home on leave in his previous letter, and his father has seized upon this in the sheer excruciating hope that his boy might be able to come home, even for just a few days. At the same time he's trying to restrain himself from sounding too excited for William's sake. He doesn't know what kind of hell he's going through, what rat-infested, shell-shaken mud bath in which he might be reading this brief connection with the life he left behind, so he tries to sound buoyant and upbeat without being flippant.

The affectionate 'old boy' at the end: William Dann is a teenager, but with this jocular light verbal punch to the upper arm Thomas Dann is talking to him adult to adult, and man to man. Finally, the addition of 'look after yourself all you can' after he's signed off. In that restrained suffix is contained every night in which Thomas had lain in the dark, wide awake, wondering where his son was and praying that he was safe. It's every moment where something around the house had reminded him of William – a shape or a glint of light catching something – the times he would have seen a flash of a familiar face in the street, a particular hair colour, or heard a laugh in a crowd and just for an instant thought, it's him, it's my Will.

Of all the poems, books and films, all the thousands of words spoken and written about the First World War, for me that 500-word missive holds all the tragedy, hope, fear and love of the war in its tiny rectangle of thin, brown, fragile paper.

As it happened, within a few weeks William Dann *was* granted leave. It was fairly unusual for a young single man to be given leave to go home, as generally the family men were considered first, but, somehow, whether his smokes were on their way or not, his number came up.

'It was wet weather, absolutely muddy, all your puttees were plastered up,' he recalled, 'then an officer came along, calling out, "Private Dann," and I said "Yes, sir," and he called out the name of another chap called Firth, and he said, "due for leave". Well, our hats nearly blew off. And we had to go, there and then, from the front-line trenches, through the reserve line, couldn't get a change of clothes, a wash, nothing.'

No chance to head off a packet of cigarettes in the post, either. 'From the transport lines we were given a paper for leave, fourteen days. We were still muddy, and they said, "You've got to get to the station as soon as you can for a train that will take you to the base." It was fifteen miles to the station and we were that tired we laid down in this field for a rest. Then Jerry came along and dropped a couple of bombs in this field and that woke us up, all right. We caught the train, got on the boat and got to London. It used to be that outside Victoria station there was a YMCA with conveniences and baths. We went in there and took off our tunics and old cardigans, and we knew they were lousy. We had a bit of a wash and I thought, that'll do till I get home. When we left there was a man shouting after us and he had our two cardigans on a stick. He said, "Oi, you two, these belong to you?" And we said, no, not ours, mate. And off I went to Brighton.

'When I got home I burnt a lot of stuff – shirt, underclothes, I couldn't burn my tunic, my father sent that to the cleaners.'

Given that the leave was dropped on William without warning, there's a good chance he hadn't been able to let his father know in advance that he was coming. In light of that letter, if it was a surprise the outpouring of emotion must have been utterly phenomenal. The days would have passed quickly – too quickly – and almost before he knew it William would have been on his way to the Front again.

'The worst part was going back,' said William. 'We met again, the same two of us, at Brighton station and caught the train to Victoria, and it was terrible, women crying, girls sobbing. We knew what we were going back to, that was the worst part. So we went outside and had a little walk around until the train was due off and that was that. We got to Folkestone and got on a boat, but apparently there was a submarine in the Channel and we had to turn round and come back into harbour, but then it was all clear and we were over in France again.'

It was two years before Fred Dixon was granted leave, but before the war was over he'd manage to get home twice.

'In the first place, you were lucky if you came home on leave at all,' he said. 'And if you did, you simply *lived* the leave. I had my first leave after two years, ten days it was, then another thirteen months later I got a fortnight. The first time, I got to Victoria station and I wanted to see a bit of London after two years away so waited for a bus to Waterloo. There was no queuing in those days; a whole crowd of people was waiting to get on and there was a mad rush. I drew back. I wasn't going to be pushed about in that mob. There was a flower seller there who caught hold of the rail of the bus, pushed the crowd back with her basket and said, "Come on, my boy, you've done your bit, you get on first." I felt proud, and very humble – yes, pride and humility, that's what it was. I said thank you very much and went up to the top deck.

'The second time I came on leave was after the Italian interlude. As I passed through the barrier at Victoria an old white-bearded man was standing there, and he raised his hat as I came through and said, "God bless you, my boy." I was quite taken aback and said, "Thank you, sir." From there I got to Woking station and was the centre of an admiring mob of American troops who wanted to know "all about it, Tommy".'

Walter Cook's leave, when it came, was a little less successful: 'On leave, the first thing I wanted to do was get out of uniform. It wasn't too clean, even after going through the thresher. The suit that I enlisted in didn't fit me any more, so I borrowed a pair of Dad's trousers and a jacket. On a corner of Stroud Green Road a girl stuck a white feather in my coat. "Thank you very much," I said, "you've made my day. I'm home on leave from the Front." She said, "Wait, are you Wally Cook?" and I said yes. She hadn't recognised me.'

Having been white-feathered, the rest of his leave was spent in the eye of the Spanish flu epidemic that was spreading across Europe: 'My aunt who lived in Knightsbridge said she heard I was home and told me her boy was seriously ill in the flu epidemic and could I come and look at him. I spent the rest of my time nursing this boy, but he died the day before I went back. Fourteen years old, he was a lovely lad. I never left him. Mother had a girl from the country, working at the Woolwich Arsenal or something – she died in bed upstairs. A bonny girl, it was as quick as that. I couldn't understand it.

'I wanted to get back. Not because I knew the way things were going and it was going to be over, but because I missed the company I'd had over there. I asked for an extension when it looked like the boy was going to pull through, but it was refused and the boy died. So I went back.'

Edward wasn't a soldier long enough to qualify for leave; the last time he would have seen his parents was probably on a couple of days' embarkation leave before he had to board the ship to cross the Channel. As he said goodbye to his parents and his younger siblings, including my grandfather, there would have been the same upbeat cheeriness expressed in Thomas Dann's letter to his son. 'I'll be back before you know it,' Edward would have reassured his mother. 'We'll see you soon,' she would have replied. 'Take care of yourself, son,' his father would have added with a handshake. And, with a pinch of my grandfather's cheek and a joke that he's practically the head of the household now so he'd better take care of things properly until he got home, Edward would have walked away, not looking back, and headed for the station. The little group at the door of number 5, Branstone Street, North Kensington would have watched him until he was out of sight, closed the door and the scene played out on thousands of doorsteps across the country would have been at an end. The gut-wrenching truth on everyone's minds would have remained unspoken.

Edward might even have thought about that day as he lay there that first night. But that was probably the last opportunity he would have had to ponder and wonder, because there was a war to win and he was there to make it happen.

16

'THE FARMHOUSE HAD TAKEN THE MAIN SHOCK OF THE BLAST, BUT THE SHACK WITH THE TWO GIRLS IN IT HAD COMPLETELY DISAPPEARED'

I took the old Ypres road from Poperinge, the road the soldiers would have taken to the front, and before long came across evidence that I really was approaching a different kind of landscape: my first military cemetery. Red Farm Military Cemetery is very small, containing fewer than fifty graves, and set back a short distance from the road in a farmer's field. I opened the gate in the low wall and entered, not really sure what to do once I had done so. I passed slowly among the neatly spaced white gravestones, reading each name – although around a quarter bore no name, just the simple inscription 'known unto God' – and noticed that all of these men had died in either April or May 1918, twenty of them on the same day, 27 April. Also bearing that date was a single stone commemorating three unnamed Belgian civilians. There was something very faintly familiar about all this, and after a short while standing among the graves I put

the Red Farm Military Cemetery and an incident recalled by Fred Dixon together. By sheer coincidence, not only did he have the answer to why so many men and the three civilians bore the same date on their headstones, but he'd actually been there.

'On 27 April, around lunchtime, we were in huts between Poperinge and Ypres on the main road,' he recalled. 'Near us was a side road leading to Dirty Bucket Camp (I think it had been taken over by the British from the French so may have been a comment on what they thought of it). On the corner of this road was a stout, well-built farmhouse and a little further up was a shack in which two girls cooked and served up plates of eggs and chips. On the other corner, facing the main road, was a casualty clearing station at the back of which was this tremendous ammunition dump. Further up the side road was a row of houses occupied by civilians.

'We were sitting on our packs in the hut eating our midday meal and suddenly the whole lot collapsed in on top of us. All these huts had been sandbagged up to three feet, and two or three rows of sandbags were on the roofs because the German airmen would occasionally fly over and machine gun the transport lines between Poperinge and Ypres. The whole lot fell on top of us, the doorway was blocked and we all had to scramble out of the top where we found the air full of iron shards and bullets, so we slid into a nearby ditch until things calmed down a bit.'

Something had caused the large ammunition dump to explode, blowing an enormous crater where it had once stood, causing chaos and carnage in the vicinity: 'At this time we were under orders to go up the line so we had to keep together – there was no question of going to help because we had no option but to keep together. Eventually we crawled away and waited until we were able to come back for our equipment. We saw that the farmhouse had taken the main shock of the blast, but the shack with the two girls in it had completely disappeared. The CCS had been demolished, as had several of the civilian houses. The crater was the size of a lake. I remember looking across and seeing, halfway down the crater on the other side, a baby's pram.

'I don't know what caused that explosion. I don't think it was a shell because we would have heard the shriek. We didn't hear a thing, other than the possible noise of an aeroplane engine. But we were busy eating our grub and used to hearing planes, so maybe a German plane had come over and the pilot had dropped a bomb on the dump. Whatever the cause, the result was tremendous.'

I came to a small clutch of graves, three rows of them, and a stone cross surrounded by a low brick wall in a field next to a road, many of which commemorated an extraordinary disaster that had killed nearly half of them on the same day. It was the first overcast day since I'd arrived in Flanders and the fields looked drab and lifeless as I stood in this small island of commemoration where the mud of everyday twenty-first century existence laps against the sanctuary of the past. A tiny plot frozen in time in which the echo of that dreadful explosion still resonates.

The oldest man in the cemetery is Alfred Rowswell, of the Royal Garrison Artillery, at forty-six. He was a docker, originally from Gravesend, who'd crossed the Thames Estuary to

Tilbury after marrying Margaret in 1906. He had two young daughters, Minnie and Kitty, and had been at war since 1914, when he was forty-two. He'd nearly made it through the whole thing. He'd had his moments: a year before his death he'd received fourteen days' field punishment for 'drunkenness and refusing to comply with an order', but then this man must have seen everything there was to see – good, bad and utterly revolting – on the Western Front. I imagined him as a large, powerful man, face craggy after years in the docks, years of bitter battle experience and middle age. He was approaching fifty and was at war alongside lads young enough to be his own sons, lads the same age as his daughters, lads like eighteen-year-old Robert Henry Thomas of the 11th Battalion, Queen's (Royal West Surrey) Regiment.

Robert, like Edward, who was only a few weeks older, would most likely have arrived in Flanders earlier that month. He was from Poplar in the East End of London, where his father, Frederick, was a commercial agent. He was the middle son, with an elder brother, Frederick, and a younger brother, Ronald. He might even have known Edward: certainly Edward would have been in the vicinity of the disaster and could even have seen the carnage, have rushed to help, ears ringing from the explosion, have recognised the faces of the dead and dying, like Robert's – whom he might even have trained with in England and come over with on the boat – heard the screams, seen the dismembered bodies among the mud and rubble, felt the helplessness and smelled the cordite, the sizzling human flesh and death.

Red Farm is a tiny cemetery, one of the smallest in the Commonwealth War Graves roster. The headstones are the customary identical white Portland stone with a curved top, regimental insignia, date of death, serial number, chiselled cross and name – names that are a gateway to a life and a story like those of Alfred Rowswell and Robert Thomas. Seventeen of these stones bore no name and were the key to no story beyond 'a soldier of the Great War': there are around 212,000 of these nameless stones among the Commonwealth war graves.

As I walked on towards Ypres I realised something else. Until now Edward had been an abstract figure, but here, for the first time, just out of Poperinge, walking the same road he'd walked, a real human being shimmered out of history to appear beside me.

Shortly after leaving Red Farm I reached Brandhoek, a hamlet so small it wasn't even marked on my map, yet this was a name familiar to me from the 10th Queen's regimental diary. In April 1918 this tiny village surrounded by fields would have been a mass of bell tents, huts, duckboards, makeshift telegraph poles and enormous camouflaged artillery beneath a sky pockmarked with observation balloons. It was practically a temporary wartime city, and the 10th Queen's were based here for a while during Edward's period of service. It was a major casualty clearing station behind the Allied lines, too – staffed in the main by some incredibly brave and dedicated Australian nurses – which explains why this tiny clutch of houses, a church and a couple of shops is home to three cemeteries housing nearly 2,000 graves.

Before long I was on the outskirts of Ypres where, while the road was otherwise clear, a man on a scooter going in the other direction chose to cross the road to my side purely in

order to give me the finger at close range. Finally, in the late
afternoon, I arrived on the western outskirts of the one town
more closely associated with the First World War than any
other in the British psyche: Ypres.

My approach would have looked very different from
Edward's. By 1918 there was very little of Ypres left standing.
Like Diksmuide, but on a larger scale, the place had been all
but completely obliterated. The Germans had been driven
out of the town during the First Battle of Ypres, in October
and November 1914, into the countryside to the north, east
and south, a situation that would remain practically static
for the next four years. In April 1915, during the Second
Battle of Ypres, the Germans tried to retake the town,
making the first use of poison gas in the history of warfare,
but saw the stalemate retained until the Third Battle of
Ypres, also known as the Battle of Passchendaele, between
July and November 1917, drove the Germans a few kilome-
tres east from Passchendaele Ridge at the cost of around half
a million lives.

Four years of shelling left this charming medieval town a
smoking ruin of rubble, splintered timber, twisted metal,
shell craters and corpses, and that's the Ypres that would
have greeted Edward when he arrived in the late spring of
1918.

The Ypres that greeted me seemed like a standard modern
Flemish town as I passed through the suburbs towards the
centre, but it's the Grote Markt that is the miracle of Ypres.
As at Diksmuide, it was decided that, instead of abandoning
the place altogether or clearing everything away and starting
from scratch, central Ypres would be rebuilt just as it had

been before the war. And before the war it was glorious: its centrepiece was the enormous, magnificent, turreted medieval Cloth Hall, completed in 1304, when Ypres' textiles were so renowned that they were exported as far as central Russia and would be mentioned in *The Canterbury Tales*. It took until 1967 for it to be fully restored when, nearly half a century after its destruction, the Cloth Hall would once again dominate central Ypres. Its rebuilding demonstrated a wonderful combination of determination and patience, and there's no greater symbol of the spirit and dignity that has embodied Ypres for centuries than when you walk into the Grote Markt and see this awe-inspiring building.

I sat and rested in the square for a while, trying to gain a feel for the place and to imagine it teeming with soldiers and horses, hearing the whistle of shells and distant – and not so distant – explosions. There was a tangibly different atmosphere here to the Grote Markt in Poperinge – for a start, it was about three times the size – and there was more urgency about Ypres than the relaxed air of 'Pops'. People seemed to be in a little more of a hurry, their heads were set at a more determined angle and their pace was quicker as they crossed the square.

Crossing the square myself I found where I was staying: Old Tom, a proper old-fashioned hotel and restaurant apparently named after a British soldier who stayed on after the war and set up a stall selling souvenirs and refreshments among the ruins and the reconstruction.

My room was up five flights of narrow, creaky wooden stairs, way up in the eaves of the building, something with which my feet made it plain they were unhappy, and I just had time to shower and change before going in search of one of Ypres' and the First World War's most poignant rituals.

There is one part of the newly ancient Ypres that isn't a reconstruction. It wasn't painstakingly rebuilt after late nights spent in the pool of a desk lamp squinting at ancient frayed-edged photographs trying to gauge the dimensions of a step-gabled dorsal roof or the curve of a medieval cornice; it wasn't using the tracing paper of history to help complete a jigsaw that was the legacy of artillery.

The Great War was not the first occasion Ypres had been under siege. The English had a go in the fourteenth century, the French tried it too and so did the Austrians, meaning that, by 1914, Ypres was practically a moated fort with ramparts. To enter or leave the eastern side of the city, the traveller used a bridge over the river between ramparts that became known as the Menenpoort. It was mainly across this bridge, with its stone lions at each end, that the Allied troops would march off to the front lines in their countless millions of boot steps, many of them making what would be a one-way journey.

Instead of reconstructing the bridge after the war, the British, who looked upon Ypres as the beating heart of their war commemoration, commissioned Reginald Bromfield to create an open-air mausoleum that straddled the road, a memorial to the thousands who'd marched east towards the sunrise, never to see it set, and who had no known resting place. Blomfield came up with the Menin Gate, a giant white stone and brick memorial – spanning the road between the old defences – classical in structure, gleaming white against the dark stone of the city and its walls.

The full task of the actual commemoration was underestimated: there are 54,896 names on the Menin Gate, all Commonwealth soldiers who lost their lives on the Ypres Salient and whose remains were never found. The thing is, those 54,896 names only take us up to 15 August 1917, when the Menin Gate ran out of space; the 34,984 men who have remained in the salient earth since that date are commemorated on a separate memorial at the enormous Tyne Cot Cemetery a few miles away.

The gate was officially unveiled on 24 July 1927, almost exactly a decade after the commencement of the mass slaughter of the Third Battle of Ypres. It didn't win universal approval: moving though its location and intention undoubtedly are, the gate is a squat, almost aggressive structure, one that Siegfried Sassoon called a 'sepulchre of crime' that would be derided by the 'doomed, conscripted, unvictorious ones' it was supposed to honour.

After nearly ninety years, however, the Menin Gate has settled into its surroundings and its daily ceremony provides the biggest and most poignant draw.

Every night, just before 8 p.m. without fail, the traffic through the gate is stopped and a small remembrance ceremony takes place, the centrepiece being the 'Last Post' played by buglers from the local volunteer fire brigade. It has happened every night at the same time since 2 July 1928, with the exception of the German occupation of the town during the Second World War. During that time the ceremony was performed at Brookwood Military Cemetery in Surrey, but the ritual began again on the very day the Poles liberated Ypres on 6 September 1944.

It was Friday evening when I left the Old Tom to make the short walk around the corner to the Menin Gate. I'd allowed the best part of half an hour before the ceremony, suspecting I would be the only person there, watching the traffic go past until a few other people wandered up, but no. As I turned out of the square and towards the gate I could see that a considerable crowd had already gathered. By the time I reached the gate it was clear the road was already closed and there were hundreds of people there. Not only that, but they were almost exclusively British people, most of them schoolchildren. I squeezed in under the arched gate, where the echo of conversational babble betrayed the high pitch of youth. There were still more than twenty minutes to go and everyone was packed in tightly. Every now and again a couple of kids would climb up the gate for a better view, only to be politely but firmly waved down by an official of the Last Post Association, which administers the nightly commemoration.

With about five minutes to go, an announcement was made requesting that people refrain from applauding either during or at the end of the ceremony. All around me the kids were chatting excitedly and messing about with their phones, scrolling through pictures with the occasional muted burst of giggles. There was one exception: a lad who was a good half a head taller than his classmates, powerfully set and pale-skinned, with dark eyes and thick curly hair that appeared to be only manageable with a set of shears. While his friends chatted and laughed around him, he looked up at the roster of names rising up the walls around him; he was motionless, his mouth slightly open, seemingly oblivious to everything going on around him as if the enormity of what was being commemorated, everything he'd been learning about at school back in England, had just hit him. To the two dimensions of the textbook a third had just been added. Of everyone there, the hundreds gathered that night, there could not have been anybody more visibly moved.

The call to attention that signalled the beginning of the ceremony was given, the hubbub died away to nothing and a forest of arms went up holding mobile phones, cameras and, in the case of a middle-aged man in front of me, a tablet computer. I couldn't see the ceremony from where I stood, but I was instead able to see the buglers in their blue uniforms lined up at the other end of the arch as tiny figures on the two dozen or so phone screens around me.

The 'Last Post' sounded, the long pause between each phrase allowing the notes to die away, echoing round the gate, bouncing around the names, falling away to a silence disturbed only by the breeze and the distant sound of traffic. After the final notes died an English voice declaimed the famous 'They shall not grow old ...' stanza of Laurence Binyon's 'For the Fallen': he placed so much emphasis on the phrase 'we *will* remember them' that his voice almost broke with the determination and emotion of the vow. The declamation commenced the minute's silence, which was immaculately observed.

After that came a procession of wreath laying, beginning with army veterans in regimental blazers and then line after disciplined line of schoolchildren, three abreast, walking solemnly forward to deposit their school's floral tributes, some in immaculate uniforms, others in jeans and hoodies, all with a dignity befitting both the occasion and the location.

Eventually, 'Reveille' sounded and the forest of arms shot up again to record the moment for posterity. After a few moments of uncertainty as to whether the ceremony was over or not, voices grew gently out of the silence and people began to melt away, making their way back to the centre. The kids rushed past me, some examining their photos and videos on their phones, others talking excitedly, a queue of them forming at an ice-cream kiosk, and then I saw the tall boy again, walking back towards the Grote Markt, hands in his jean pockets, alone, looking at the ground and absolutely lost in thought.

Some aspects of the occasion had made me uncomfortable: the need for an announcement to prevent people applauding and the massed raising of audio-visual technology at the crucial moments made me wonder whether I'd been at a commemoration or a performance. I feared that if the modern culture of conspicuous compassion – of the sort that has spittle-flecked buffoons writing in to complain about television presenters not wearing poppies, and sees people applauding a commemoration ceremony and turning the 'Last Post' into video fodder like the Changing of the Guard at Buckingham Palace – had reached the Menin Gate, then we'd learned little over the previous century. The passing of the Great War from memory to history had seen commemoration turned into a show.

But then I asked myself, What was I doing here? As far as I was aware, I had nobody commemorated on the Menin

Gate; I was there for no other reason than the fact that you couldn't go to Ypres without seeing the 'Last Post' ceremony, in the same way that you couldn't go to Rome without seeing the Coliseum. For all my respectful intentions and the commemorative motivation for my journey I was just a tourist motivated by curiosity. The coach-loads of school-children were there to lay wreaths, most likely to former pupils commemorated there: they had more right to be at the gate than I did, and who was I to roll my eyes at them recording the thing on their phones? The silence had been properly observed – that was all that mattered.

I emerged from my introspection as I reached the Grote Markt and saw the tall boy again, looking past me back in the direction of the gate with an expression of wonder. I turned and saw that the setting sun had bathed the white stone of the gate in the deepest, most beautiful orange light. The day had been overcast and this was the first time the sun had appeared, enriching the Menin Gate with a stunning display of colour.

I sat outside a bar on the square, ordered a beer and watched the rest of the sunset make silhouettes of the spires and turrets of the Cloth Market and town hall, the western sky a blaze of orange, pink and purple. At a table near me a group of men, the top buttons of their white shirts undone and regimental ties loosened, raised their glasses in a solemn toast and, at the going down of the sun, remembered the men they'd come here to commemorate.

It was only the next morning that it truly dawned on me how everyone in Ypres seemed to be British. It was spring and the tourist season was still some way off, yet the Grote

Markt, the shops, even the breakfast room at the Old Tom all resonated with accents from across the Channel. At a table near me, four middle-aged men with wire-framed glasses, neat moustaches, Home Counties accents and a definite whiff of the rugby club bar about them consulted carefully planned printed itineraries over their coffee, and when a wiry man in a polo shirt stood up from his table and addressed Christine, the maternally warm hostess at the Old Tom, with a broad Glaswegian 'ahll peffertherumeinaweeminnit, kayhen?', her smiling assent revealed she had clearly understood that he would settle his accommodation bill shortly if that suited, madam.

After breakfast I went to have a proper look at the Menin Gate. The road from the Grote Markt to the gate is populated with battlefield tour offices and souvenir shops offering everything from the shell and bullet casings still being ploughed up from the surrounding fields by local farmers to bottles of calvados with a drawing of a First World War trooper on the label and jewellery 'made with real poppies'.

I went in to one shop as the proprietor handed a man a plastic bag containing whatever souvenirs he'd just bought. 'Thank you,' said the man, trousering his change before lowering his head and adding solemnly, 'I had to buy something from you.' In Ypres, even the purchase of a fridge magnet can be imbued with the gravity of remembrance, it seems.

I surprised myself by pausing only briefly at the Menin Gate. Having heard the 'Last Post' dying away among the towering lists of names the previous evening and seen it lit flaming orange by the sunset, perhaps the traffic passing

through it and trickles of pedestrians on their way somewhere lent it an underwhelming, workaday aspect. I stayed
for a couple of minutes reading some of the names, but here
on a Saturday morning, without any sense of ceremony as
the breeze ruffled the previous evening's wreaths, forlorn
without the gravity of silence around them, I found I was
soon keen to move on.

I climbed the stairs next to the gate that led on to the
ramparts and headed south. It was a beautiful morning and,
as I was staying a second night at the Old Tom, I didn't have
a heavy rucksack on my back and a new place to be by the
end of the day. I dallied. I sat on benches and let the sun
warm my face. I examined the information boards about the
history of the ramparts that showed there is more to Ypres
than a nightly ceremony and the First World War, but any
other aspect of Ypres is always going to be a daisy struggling
beneath a rosebush.

As I came around the south side of the ramparts, crossing
the Lille Gate, I found what must be the most beautiful
cemetery on the whole of the Western Front. I've not seen
many, admittedly, but there can't possibly be a more exqui-
sitely placed collection of the fallen than the Ramparts
Cemetery. It slopes gently towards the town's moat, where
willow trees dip their branches into the water. The headstones – 198 men are buried here – all face out towards the
moat in terraced rows like guardian sentries awaiting a foe
that will never come.

I felt a genuine sense of peace here. I walked slowly among
the stones, in which there are irregular gaps, presumably
from when the French soldiers who once lay here were

exhumed and repatriated. Yet some of the headstones are slotted together side by side, shoulder to shoulder, like a row of teeth: the men were all from the same regiment and died on the same day. I sat for while looking across the stones to the tranquil water beyond and thought about what a beautiful place this was in which to spend your eternal rest. A century earlier, of course, there would have been no beauty here at all. What Edward saw here couldn't have been more different.

17

'I WASN'T SCARED ADVANCING. AS FAR AS I REMEMBER THERE WAS JUST A BLIND ACCEPTANCE THAT WE WERE GOING FORWARD AND THAT WAS THAT'

The early days of Edward's war are fairly easily pieced together from other accounts. Charles Ward, for example, also arrived on the Western Front in the spring of 1918, after serving in Ireland, and his experiences would have been standard for lads like him. Almost as soon as he arrived, Charles was preparing for an attack east of Ypres on a low ridge called Triangular Bluff.

'In April 1918 we arrived in the Ypres sector and went on a firing course,' he said, 'but I'm afraid we weren't very good at firing .303 rifles. Finally we marched through Ypres to our front-line trenches at Zillebeke Lake, a rather nasty place a couple of miles south-east of Ypres. Not that the place was attacked specifically, but they were always throwing over 5.9 shells: on one occasion they threw over nearly sixty in one go.

'There'd been fighting there on and off throughout the war: the whole area was just mud waste except around Ypres itself, where a gentleman by the name of Warrington had built a road made of railway sleepers that ran right through the immediate area of the Ypres ramparts. On the side of this road was the Lille Gate, which dated back to ancient times. Just inside the gate there was a place we called Dirty Bucket Camp, where we used to have spray baths: you undressed and went under a spray from over your head. We went there fairly regularly that spring, and I had more baths there in a few days than the whole time I was in France.

'The bridge by the Lille Gate at the south end of the Ypres city wall was an ancient bridge, but it was made ready to be blown up in case of an emergency. As we were going to finally advance they decided to take away the charges. Two Royal Engineers got underneath to remove the charges and blew themselves and the bridge up. Further along, the swamp in front of the ramparts was a mass of muddy water, probably six–eight feet deep.'

This was roughly the location of the Ramparts Cemetery today.

'Not long after arriving we had to go into the front line at Zillebeke Lake, south-east of the town. The other companies were on our right and we did turns of duty between the lake and the main road leading into Ypres. In the middle of the day a German aeroplane used to come over and we had to get under cover – a hole in a trench with a top covered with timber and corrugated iron and just a small dugout, enough to take two people. There was just an odd number of those about and that's where we'd go.

'Most days Zillebeke Lake got a few shells over. The Germans seemed to think our trench was very important, probably because we were the only people between the Germans and the capture of Ypres, so it was a very important place. The trench wasn't pleasant but you got used to it in time. Previously, the big battles had taken place miles away – the end of the Menin Road, four or five miles away – but in the Spring Offensive the Germans had driven us back until we were almost on top of Ypres. There were only about 700 men between Ypres and the Germans, but we'd made up our minds that they weren't going to get any further.

'I not only dealt with the front line work, but very often I was sent back behind the lines to places like Poperinge to get cigarettes and chocolate. On one occasion I went back to Pop and visited Toc H [Talbot House] and had a nice meal of egg, chips and coffee with bread and butter, probably the first time I'd had anything like that for about six weeks.'

Charles appeared to have a built-in survival instinct: 'One day in around September, I was taking a message towards what we called Café Belge crossroads not long before we were due to attack Triangle Bluff, when for no apparent reason I suddenly grabbed hold of the other runner who was with me, lifted him up and threw him down into a trench and jumped in myself. Almost immediately a shell burst three or four yards away from us. Had I not thrown him in, we would both have been killed. I must have heard it coming. It was a famous crossroads on the right of Ypres, full of shell holes. No buildings anywhere, everything was destroyed. When we got there it was one great big shell hole and we soon got that filled in. It was necessary to do that to get ready for the attack. The shell holes in the roads had to be filled in otherwise traffic couldn't have gone along then.'

To open the attack the Belgian artillery laid down a colossal bombardment, and Charles was part of the second wave of the advance, following the front line troops. They found only token opposition, were able to take the bluff and the German positions without a great deal of resistance and suffered few casualties.

'One of the German dead there was one of the largest men I've ever seen in my life. He was lying on a mound just inside the bluff and he was really huge; I've never seen anything quite like it,' he remembered.

'Having taken the dugouts, the battalion headquarters went into them and it wasn't long before the one-legged brigadier came along and gave a wonderful exhibition of kissing all and sundry on both cheeks. He was a marvellous fellow, I can't remember his name; we didn't worry about names in those days. I never knew the names of the officers. The whole thing was so fluid, you see.

'Our first-aid man was an Irishman we called Paddy. Because he was angry about one of our men being killed, he threatened blue murder for any German we met. I went out to find his post on the following morning and found him in a big lavatory box, and there he was, looking after a little tiny Saxon who had a broken shoulder, and he was attending to this German and he was swearing at the top of his voice at the British Army for leaving the little chap out in the rain all night.'

In most of the accounts, I found almost without exception that the British Tommies bore little malice towards their German equivalents. Soldier to soldier, man to man, there seemed to be no particular antagonism. There was a definite psychological dichotomy between the Germans, the Hun, the baby-bayoneting man-demons in the spiked helmets, and the Germans, the regular blokes with wives, sweethearts and jobs at home who were just doing their bit for their country.

'I think the chaps we fought were the average man, really,' said William Dann. 'They were in their army and they had to do a job the same as we did, man to man and the best man won. They were good soldiers in general. We used to say all sorts of remarks when we shot them, "That's got the buggers," but then it passed out of your head until the next lot.'

Bill Holmes from Battersea was a nineteen-year-old private in the London Regiment. He too bore no personal malice for the individual German soldier, even after a close encounter during a trench raid to capture a sentry.

'We were as quiet as we could be,' he said. 'It was a pitch-black night. We could see the sentry, made a rush for him and soon overpowered him. Three lads were left guarding him while the other five of us ran quickly along the trench, throwing our bombs into the dugouts. Any Germans we saw we'd just throw a bomb at him. It was pandemonium, a question of seconds; we had to race down those trenches and get rid of our bombs. We couldn't go back until we'd got rid of all our bombs.

'The Germans had seen the sentry had been captured so they were getting in touch with their artillery, and troops were converging on where we were and they were shooting at us. Luckily, as far as I can remember none of us were hit. The sentry knew there was nothing he could do so he just came with us back through the wire and across no man's land. Of course, while that was going on a barrage was being laid down all along our line. I think in the end there were three casualties out of our eight.

'The sentry was handed over to our officer, and he was taken straight away to the colonel's office for interrogation. We certainly wouldn't bully the prisoner. There was no animosity; we just thought they were men doing a job the same as we were, defending their country.'

In most of these accounts of life in the trenches there is rarely any mention of fear. In thinking about Edward during his first days at the Front, I assumed he must have been scared, because I know I would have been. Whether he was a reluctant soldier or one itching for a crack at the Hun, he must, surely, have been frightened, especially at first.

'I felt frightened many a time,' said Charles Ward, 'especially when things were going up close at hand, but I never dwelt on it. I saw chaps crying, chaps with shell shock, crying for their mother, praying, all that kind of thing. You'd console them and help them along, but there wasn't much you could do. They'd come around, I suppose.'

Bill Holmes seemed inured to the experience: 'You never knew when the bombardments were coming, night or day. They could last for hours, during which time you could do nothing but sit there and wait for yours to hit you. You'd see bits of bodies, whole bodies, arms, legs, all up in the air when a shell hit. Then when it was over you had to repair the damage and rebuild the trench again. The shells that worried us most were ones that we named rum jars. We'd see them coming towards us but they wouldn't come in a direct line, so you wouldn't know where they were going to land. They were the most terrifying thing. There was no use running because there was every chance you'd run to the place where it would land. They were zigzagging all over the place.

'But you get past being terrified. Your whole mentality is geared to take what's coming and put up with it. That's why discipline was so essential, otherwise men would just jump over the top and run away.'

In that spring of 1918, Bill himself witnessed first hand what happened when fear got the better of discipline among young recruits just arrived at the Front: 'We were always getting new recruits from London, and one day these two lads arrived who could have been no more than sixteen. They'd been with us for two weeks when we had to make an attack on a German position, after they'd captured an entire battalion of ours. When they realised they would be taking part in the attack these two youngsters were literally crying their eyes out, and when we went up to attack there was no sign of them, they'd cleared off. They were caught by the redcaps three or four miles away and charged with desertion.

'On the Sunday, the whole battalion was paraded on the large parade ground, even the cooks. The two young men were brought in and their caps and insignia were torn off them. Then the verdict was read out, how these two young men had deserted and by their desertion they would be shot at dawn the next day. It was decided that the men from the same platoon, including me, would draw lots to be part of the four-man execution squad. The numbers were put into a bag and luckily I wouldn't be one of the squad. Those four men knew what they had to do the next morning and they were almost sick with the whole thought of it, shooting their own mates.

'The next morning, these two lads were brought out to the yard and blindfolded. The four men were each told which of the boys to take; one was to fire at the boy's head, the other at his heart so they'd be killed instantly. It was awful. Their parents were never told they'd been executed, they were just sent a telegram telling them they'd been killed on active service. The four men were almost sick when they got back. I don't think they could eat all day.

'We felt sympathy for the two boys, but we had more sympathy for the parents. It was a terrible thing. We lived with the thought of that for weeks and weeks. But you're warned about it, you know you can be shot for desertion and even for disobeying an officer. It was the only thing that could be done.'

Walter Cook was also in the area in the spring of 1918 when the Allies began to push the Germans back. While there, he struck up a friendship that would stay with him for the rest of his life: 'We were near the River Lys, and the Germans were starting to resist violently our strategic points. We had an idea they were beginning to crack but somehow it seemed hard to believe because the casualties were mounting up and our dressing of the wounded was almost at its peak.

'We lost men ourselves. There was the same feeling in the ambulance corps as there was in the army itself because, as we lost our volunteers from 1914, we were sent conscripted men who were sometimes near-conscientious-objector types. The same spirit and dash that our original lads had wasn't always there.

'There was one exception, though. One newly arrived stretcher-bearer, Orlando, an Italian, couldn't have been much older than I was and for some reason he thought I should learn to play chess. He had a chess set of which I've never seen the like since. He had a cardboard black and white board with slots at the end of each square and into these slots cardboard figures went. I think he'd made it himself. He'd teach me how to play on it whenever we'd come across each other. His cardboard set folded in two and just fitted into his jacket pocket so we could resume the game the next time we met, when he'd single me out, raise an eyebrow and say, "Game of chess?" Of course, we got bullied by comrades – "Oh, they're at it again, everyone be quiet" – but we didn't mind. He didn't play in a serious way; he always had a joke. If he was going to move a knight, he'd say "Now, this is a *courtly* knight": he had a yarn for every move. I never won a game but I did enjoy it, and I enjoyed his company because he was a humourist.

'I was very sorry when he was shot. The chaps with him on his unit sent me his chess set but I lost it when I was bombed out in London. I was very upset about that. In later years someone gave me a wonderful chess set, but it wasn't a patch on this cardboard one. What a wonderful chap he must have been to think it up.'

Across the Front such nascent friendships were being snuffed out before being allowed to flicker fully into life, and good-news stories seemed scarce. For Walter Cook, though, there was to be a significant moment of redemption: 'The reason I went to help was that Uncle Bob said men were left to die because they were fighting a retreat, and there was nobody there to help. One day, Captain Hancock came in and said, "You four chaps come along, will you? A working party's gone out and I want you to go over the top and see if you can find anybody because there are four men missing."

'We went to the line. It was night-time and the star shells were going up at intermittent intervals. I was shown where to go over, and over I went, helped by a lusty sergeant, to a stretch of no man's land about 80 yards long, when the gap between the lines here was about 500 yards. To be in front of your own infantry with an armband on to look for somebody who might be wounded was a dangerous task, but up I went and when a star shell went up I stood still and when it went down I moved about. When a German light went up, suddenly I saw about 40 yards away what I thought looked like a huddled figure lying on the ground. Even in such a dangerous location it struck me: this is why I'm here, he's been left to die, just like Bob said. When the light had gone out, carefully I made my way towards this bundle and it was a wounded Scotsman. Just as I reached him an officer appeared, saying he'd come to help. We put this chap on a groundsheet, put field dressings on his wounds and got him back to the line. I think Uncle Bill would have been pleased about that because that's exactly why I was out there.

'The Scotsman was evacuated to the CCS, dressed, sent home and, after the war, many years later, I went to a reunion in Glasgow – and there he was. He was the porter at the hotel where the reunion was taking place. He said that the 27th Field Ambulance will never have a reunion in any other hotel as long as he lived because we'd appeared and brought him in from no man's land when he'd thought all was lost.

'I never knew his name.'

Alan Short had been wounded in the arm and sent back to England, returning to the Front in August 1918, drafted to the 2/8th Post Office Rifles: 'A cousin and a friend had been killed serving with that battalion, so I wasn't very happy about it.'

Despite his reservations, he soon found himself back in the old routine, improvising and making do: 'You had two hours on duty, keeping watch and probably tidying up and repairing the trenches. Off duty you'd sleep. There were very few dugouts in the trenches. If you were lucky there was a bit of corrugated iron to put over the trench for a bit of shelter, but only if you were lucky.

'At night you would go out on patrol. I think I was more frightened there than at any other time, getting lost and that. Usually three or four of you would go out and listen for enemy patrols, and when Verey lights went up you either fell down and kept still or hoped that they just took you for a tree stump. On patrols I worried I'd be taken prisoner; that was the main thing that concerned me. But overall, you accepted the conditions – you were under orders and you obeyed them. To my mind you had no decisions to make yourself, you were told what to do and you did it. I wasn't scared advancing. As far as I remember there was just a blind acceptance that we were going forward and that was that. It was only when I heard the church bells that I started wondering how many of us would hear them the next morning.'

Fully supplied with cigarettes, William Dann was also just getting on with it: 'We never gave a thought to losing the war. I thought eventually we should get through them. And, of course, the Americans came in eventually, and that made a difference because we were getting short of military age men. I saw quite a bit of the American troops. The first time was when we were coming out of the front line as they were going in. As one went past he said, "Hallo Tommy, where's this shooting gallery we're heading for?" and all that sort of chat. I thought, "You'll soon find it about half a mile up the way, mate." They seemed quite normal chaps, like us.'

Such banter may have been fine private to private, but the wrong quip at the wrong time at the wrong person's expense could land a man in serious trouble.

'We were going up from Ypres to the Menin Gate this particular night,' said William. 'It was fairly quiet and there were some sappers working on our left on the way up, mining or something. Just as we got there, next to an officer on horseback, somebody shouted up, "Can you chuck us down that bit of board, mate?" My number two, he was a bit cheeky and he said, "Which bits do you want, mate, the bit with the monkey on or the other bit?" The officer heard it, took his name and he was tied to the wheel of a GS wagon as punishment. Actually strapped onto this wheel by the redcaps. There was shell fire coming over and we all kicked up such a stink about it that he was eventually released, but he had extra latrine duties and things for a while.'

It was an experience that would have been familiar to Bill Holmes. His battalion was marched back from the lines to take part in a practice attack in preparation for a major advance: the terrain to which they were taken was similar to that of the real location. On arrival, Bill was tasked with distributing the dummy ammunition to the rest of the men.

As he recalled: 'My sergeant said, "Bill, I want you to go round to all the chaps with this big bag of dummy cartridges." So off I went. There were so many men to give these things to it was quite a time before I got back to my place and my own rifle, and just as I was putting the last dummy round in the magazine the sergeant suddenly barked out, "Ready to attack!" It so frightened me that I jumped and accidentally pulled the trigger. It made such a noise, everybody was looking round. The brigadier who'd been inspecting the troops galloped up on his horse, pointed at me and said, "Put that man under close arrest." My two mates had to fix bayonets, take away my rifle and march me 300 yards back to where the cooks were. The cooks had to take charge of me until we got back to the billets again.

'As soon as I got to my billet I was sent to the officer commanding who said to me, "Look, I've been ordered by the brigadier to charge you, because if it had been the real thing and your rifle went off like that, the Germans would have heard that shot and it would have given the whole game away. I've been told to charge you with the worst punishment you could possibly have – you're going to be spread-eagled on a gun wheel for two hours, once a day, for seven days." My sergeant tried to get it annulled but the commander said he was very sorry, but it was the brigadier's instructions.'

It sounds today like an astonishingly harsh punishment, but Bill Holmes was sanguine about it, even years later.

'I didn't feel it was unfair,' he said. 'When I considered what I'd done and it had been explained to me that I would have prejudiced the whole attack, I could honestly only agree that I fully deserved whatever punishment they gave me. I was taken by the sergeant up to where the redcaps had their HQ, where they had this big old gun. The sergeant told me what was going to happen and, as I stood there, he tied one of my legs with wire, then the other, then both hands were tied on at the wrists, spread-eagled across this gun wheel. I had to stay in that position for two hours and it was a terrible feeling. Not absolute agony or anything like that, but it was damned uncomfortable.

'Luckily for me, when they came and released me and I was taken to the redcaps' office, the sergeant said, "Bill, we feel that you've had quite enough. I'm going to fill in the form that says you'll have done seven days but you needn't come any more." I could hardly believe it was true.'

As Edward got used to the routines and rhythms of life on the front line, the 10th Queen's prepared to join the advance that would push the Germans back across the very land they'd taken during the Spring Offensive – and ultimately win the war. He would almost certainly have come across Fred Dixon, whose account makes it pretty clear when Edward would have arrived.

'After the advance of the Germans, the 10th Queen's were on the Kemmel front, south-west of Ypres, on a little pimple of a hill called the Scherpenberg,' he said. 'The Germans had captured Kemmel, which was slightly higher than where we were and meant we were under observation all day long. There was a slope from Scherpenberg to the foot of Kemmel, and our troops were facing them in foxholes and strongpoints all along the valley. At the time we arrived we were just five officers and 374 other ranks after leaving the Somme. We had to wait for reinforcements of twenty officers and 577 other ranks, and then we were put in front of Kemmel, where Jerry was hoping to catch the remaining hills between us and the coast.'

I'm fairly certain that Edward would have been among those 577.

Fred had become a specialist linesman, an important job in any army but especially one on the move: without telephone communication the battalions had a difficult job knowing who was where, who should be where and who should be going where.

'We were in dugouts on the Scherpenberg,' he recalled, 'and our telephone line ran down the face of the hill to the company in the valley. The hours of darkness were the only times you could do any work outside, and for the linesmen repairing lines, that was the busiest part of the day as much as for anyone else: trench digging, ration parties, patrols, all those things had to be carried out at night. Both sides knew this was happening, and shelling and machine gunning went on all night, and we came in for a lot of it.

'If a line goes down, the linesman stumbles along in the dark with the line in his hand till he comes to the break. He places it where he can find it again, then goes further on to where the line should be and pulls in the loose end. Then, if he's lucky, he has sufficient loose wire to join the ends. It wasn't a job everybody would like, but you were your own boss and that's why I liked it. Sometimes while you were out, the Germans would put a barrage of 5.9s on the slope and you'd hear a machine gun sweeping all the way around, at which point the wisest thing to do was get into a shell hole. Often you'd hear the bullets cutting the grass over your head. One time I was out there, the machine gun corps shouted to me, "Don't be such a bloody fool, get down out of it." But the funny thing is, you only become aware of the danger when you've moved out of the danger, rather than when you're actually up top.

'On this particular occasion I had to take a message to the commander of C Company down in the valley. It was quiet, there was no moon and everything was peaceful. Too peaceful, really, and sure enough I was checked by a whisper, "Halt, who's there?" I was in no man's land and had come across one of our patrols. I replied "QUJ", meaning 10th Queen's. "Give me the password," said the voice. "I don't know the bloody password," I said. "The day of the week," said the voice. "I don't know the bloody day of the week, either," I had to reply. You never troubled about what day of the week it was. The date, yes, as a signaller you had to know the date, but not what day it was. It was a barmy password

'Later that day, we were inside a tunnel burrowed deep into the Scherpenberg, a U-shaped tunnel that had little offices on one side. In order to keep the place ventilated they had a hand-driven pump, and the personnel had to man this pump twenty-four hours, and signallers, runners, intelligence people, everybody had to take their half-hour shift grinding this pump. One day I went outside for a breath of fresh air on the side away from Kemmel. I saw a salvo of shells fall in the hollow lying between Kemmel and

Reningelst, where I knew one of our companies was situated, and a sergeant major friend of mine called Stan Dale was there. I wondered if he was all right, having seen these shells going off, but that night Stan came up to the battalion HQ and I saw him. I mentioned having seen these shells and he told me what had happened. A few weeks earlier, a draft of nineteen-year-old boys had come out from England, known as "A4 Boys" …'

Officially, a soldier had to be nineteen years old before being sent to the Front. After the huge losses caused by the German Spring Offensive, the rule was relaxed, and boys aged between eighteen and a half and nineteen were shipped out. These lads were classed as 'A4' and hence became the 'A4 Boys'. Edward Connelly would turn nineteen on 25 April 1918 so would have been an A4 Boy. This reference by Fred Dixon, combined with Edward's will, dated 2 April, convinces me that Edward arrived at the Front in early April to shore up the Queen's' numbers after their dreadful losses.

'One of the A4 lads had chummed up with an older man, who'd been in the battalion for some time,' said Fred. 'The salvo of shells I'd seen had come over and that's where the friendship stopped. His pal, the older man, knelt down beside him and said, "Pray, chum, pray," but the young chap was too far gone to do anything. The older man said, "Gentle Jesus, meek and mild, look upon a little child. Pity my simplicity, suffer them to come to thee. Amen." And the lad died.

'As was usual, the sergeant major and this man began to go through the lad's pockets for his personal effects to send home. Stan was just getting his wristwatch and the older man had gone for his paybook. Suddenly, from behind them they heard a man shout, "No!" They looked round and could see the man was quite white and very upset. Stan asked him what the matter was. He said, "Good God, sergant major, that boy's my son." Apparently, several years before, he'd left his wife with a baby boy and they'd only just met again, by chance, at Kemmel a few days earlier.'

18

'THE SURGEON COULDN'T FIND THE BULLET AND I WAS IN AGONY, SO THEY GAVE ME A CUP OF TEA AND GAVE ME HEROIN'

When Edward arrived at the front – most likely on 14 April – the 10th Queen's were in the line just north-east of Ypres in the Passchendaele sector, a particularly unpleasant sea of mud, shell holes filled to the brim with brown water, shattered hulks of destroyed tanks, wrecked and splintered field guns, and the occasional hand or boot of a corpse poking out of the ground, all for as far as the eye could see. He and his fresh-faced colleagues would have arrived just in the nick of time, too: the bigwigs, in their wisdom, had decided this sector of some 2,200 yards of the line should be only lightly held and took some of the troops away to place elsewhere. This left the beleaguered Queen's to hold a stretch of front line that should have been manned by two battalions, rather than one shattered, depleted and disheartened one. Two days later, the German capture of the hill at Kemmel saw the Allied lines withdrawn closer to Ypres, and the 10th Queen's slipped quietly back towards the eastern ramparts of the town under cover of darkness, holding a 1,200 yard stretch of the St Jean

Road close to the ramparts of north-eastern Ypres. William Dann remembered the arrival of Edward and his colleagues.

'A lot of the chaps were a bit demoralised,' he said. 'When we got a bit organised again we were sent back to Passchendaele and Ypres with new recruits. It wasn't so bad, really, but it was bad enough. We only had to hold the lines, and we were to and fro between Passchendaele and Ypres.'

Wilfred Heavens was in the same part of the line around the same time and gives an idea of the some of the sights Edward might have seen. One evening in May, Heavens was making his way to the front line to the north of Ypres.

'The Germans were shelling the road,' he said. 'There was a right turn called Salvation Corner that was always heavily shelled by the Germans. Just up the road behind a hedge was stationed a battery of our field guns, which now and then opened fire, lighting up parts of the road in front of us. Where the column of troops reached the corner, they swerved suddenly from the side of the road to the centre to avoid what proved to be the dead bodies of two soldiers lying huddled at the side of the road. On the opposite side stood a wagon with two horses harnessed in the shafts. One lay on the ground in agony, bleeding from a big wound in its side, and the other stood upright, apparently unhurt but trembling all over with fright. The rattling of the harness could be heard down the road. Everybody was passing as quickly as possible and did not appear to have the time, or care about releasing the uninjured horse and doing away with the injured one.'

Not long afterwards, Heavens was making his way to the front line for a routine tour of duty: 'While marching through the communication trench, on our way the enemy suddenly opened fire, and in a moment the trench was full of casualties. Those who were not hit jumped out of the trench and made their way as fast as they could to the support line. The stretcher-bearers were left with the wounded, who were groaning and calling to us to help them. The first man I came to was lying face down at the bottom of the trench; he was unconscious and had a large wound in his back, near his shoulder. The inside flesh was protruding, which I gently poked back with my finger and put a bandage on. We carried him to the dressing station but he was dead on arrival. We were busy all night clearing the trench of the dead and wounded.'

A few days later, Heavens was present at another surprise German artillery attack on the trenches with devastating consequences: 'Suddenly, without the slightest warning, the Germans dropped a barrage right on the trench, shelling along its whole length. Practically every shell was a direct hit; the men stood no chance whatsoever and were slaughtered wholesale. The sides of the trench were blown in and men were killed and buried at the same time. Some were blown out of the trench, quite ten yards away, others had limbs blown off. The bearers, who were at the extreme end of the company, were quite unhurt.

'We climbed out of the trench and ran along the top, searching for wounded. The first man we reached was a platoon officer, Lieutenant Washington. He was seriously injured and before we reached the dressing station he succumbed to his wounds. We were up and down to the dressing station all night. Out of thirty-odd wounded, only four reached the dressing station alive. Those who had succumbed to their wounds were laid out in a line outside the door of the dressing station. Those who were killed outright were in too bad a condition to remove and were covered over where they lay. Some were never found. We knew the spot where they had been working, and all we could see was a filled-in trench and blackened, burnt earth.'

So, although this was a relatively quiet time on the Ypres front, it would have been clear to Edward that disaster and tragedy could be only a second away. For the rest of the time, however, life was quiet and filled with the familiar routines and unique rhythms of life at the Front. Bill Holmes described how days passed in the trenches, away from raids, shelling and gas attacks: 'Even in the line you had to shave every morning, and the only thing you had to shave with was your tea, so you had to leave enough tea to make sure you could shave. In the afternoons you'd sit there discussing your families, where you lived and so on. You weren't allowed to get into groups in the trenches, though, in case a shell came over, so you'd all be about two or three yards from each other. Near the firing line you always had to be in single file in case of shelling, so there would be less damage. For dinner they'd come along with a Dixie, a big pan with a handle, full of stew. Each man would get a couple of ladles into his mess tin, then a Dixie of tea would be brought out. You kept your mess tin clean with mud and water. As soon as night fell you'd just go into your dugout because it was pitch dark and there was nothing you could do.'

'The rations were terrible,' recalled James Watson. 'There wasn't enough bread and you mostly got bully beef and biscuits. The saying was that they built trenches on bully beef. The biscuits were rock hard, two or three inches square. There were lads with false teeth who couldn't cope with the biscuits. The lice got into your food as well, in your spoonful of jam and even in the bully beef stew. In the winter you got two spoonsful of rum to keep you warm. It used to come in stone bottles. One time there were two soldiers who'd been missing for a couple of days, and one night a work party went out to no man's land to put barbed wire out and they found these two lads out there with one of these jars, blind drunk.'

In June the 10th Queen's returned to the front at Oudezeele, a village west of Poperinge, with a new commanding officer, Colonel Edward Bunbury North. North was forty-eight years old and a hugely experienced soldier from a colonial military background, having seen service in Egypt, South Africa and Japan. He took the battalion to the hill at Scherpenberg, expecting heavy fighting, but with the German advance having run out of steam the Queen's only saw occasional action and suffered a handful of casualties.

While things remained relatively quiet throughout the summer, the battalion took part in occasional raids on German positions, one of which earned a Military Cross for Lieutenant Girling, for managing to capture a German officer. It wouldn't be until the end of September that the Queen's were put into action again. In the meantime, Edward and his colleagues witnessed a remarkable aerial encounter, recalled by Fred Dixon.

'Some time during July or August, I found myself at the transport line of the battalion at Brandhoek, between Ypres and Poperinge, where we were billeted,' he said. 'At this time, the Germans used to send planes over to shoot up the transport lines, but this generally only happened during the hours of darkness. So it was with some surprise that we saw a plane carrying the familiar black crosses in daylight coming from the direction of Ypres, passing over the top of us and flying on towards Poperinge. We soon twigged its purpose: behind "Pop" were a number of observation balloons, probably eight in all, winched high into the sky to keep an eye on what was happening behind the German lines. They must also have been suspicious of activities behind our lines, because they had approximately the same number of balloons up in the vicinity of Menin.'

I imagined Edward standing among the bell tents at Brandhoek, possibly with Fred, looking up at the plane and seeing the dark puffs of anti-aircraft fire bursting around it in the clear summer sky, shielding his eyes from the sun with his hand, watching the plane head west towards the first of the British observation balloons.

'The winchers on the tenders got to work to have them down, but it was to no avail. The Boche sent first one down in flames, then another and another, until all eight of them had been shot down in huge fireballs. We saw two figures jumping from each basket and some of their parachutes opened in time, others didn't. Fragments from the burning bags of gas fell on more than one of the opened parachutes, which in turn blazed in mid-air and caused the parachutist to fall to the ground.

'We were all hopping mad. But then, from the south, one of our planes appeared bearing the red, white and blue roundels of the Royal Air Force. How we cheered when we saw him, particularly when, after a brief encounter, the Boche bailed out of his plane and landed on a roof somewhere in Poperinge.

'To our intense satisfaction our flier then turned east and made a beeline for Ypres, then passed over the German lines. Bursts of AA traced his course, but he made straight for the German balloons, which began to haul down as soon as they realised what was going on. From that distance he was just a little black dot, but we saw first one balloon burst into flames, then another and so on, until he had entirely cleared the skies of Boche balloons. We prayed for his safety as he turned for home followed by bursts of gunfire. He came over Ypres and Brandhoek and we cheered like madmen till he had passed over us.'

During the same period, Fred was involved in a bizarre incident designed to boost the morale of … well, it wasn't entirely clear: 'When we were on the march, some wag would start up singing "We won't be buggered about, we won't, we won't be buggered about" and that would be taken up by the whole battalion. On 4 August, I consider we really were buggered about. On the night of the 2nd, all the old soldiers were taken out of the line, old soldiers according to service. I was one of them and we all received the 1915 ribbon. Then we were taken down to transport lines. The next day was spent having a bath and being given fresh clothes. Well, I say fresh, they'd been fumigated after being used by someone else and the lice eggs were still in them. Then we had to put in a lot of shining and polishing of our equipment and had orders to parade early the next morning with side arms and bayonets. We were then told to proceed without our greatcoats to a light railhead, where we got on board some open trucks and were taken to a village several miles away, marched up the street, halted and told to fall out and "look natural". Of course, everyone made for the nearest estaminet, especially as then it started to rain. Then we were given the bizarre order to fall in and look at rest. Well, we did our best. Then Captain Goring said, "In a very short while, round the corner of that street will come a car and King George will be in it. When he drives past us and I put my cap up in the air, I want you all to give him a cheer."

'Well, it was raining and miserable, we'd been told we wouldn't need our greatcoats and we hadn't even had time for a drink, so the mood wasn't particularly jolly. After a little while the car came round the corner. Up went Captain Goring's hat, and not a man cheered. It was a proper flop. King George sat in this open car, and he looked as miserable as sin. Goring was a bit annoyed. He said, "When the king comes back in about three quarters of an hour, I want you to put on a better show." But exactly the same thing happened. We didn't cooperate: we were being buggered about. It was all eyewash.

'We went back in our trucks, our new equipment was taken away, we were given our old stuff back and taken back up to the line. B Company went over the top the next morning and one of them, Woods, his name was, an Irishman who'd been at Mons, was killed. He wasn't killed in the offensive when the men went over the top. They were beaten back but left behind several wounded. Woods got back over our side of the embankment but could hear a chap stuck on the other side, moaning. He said, "I can't stand this any longer," so he got up, got to the top of the bank and was shot through the head.'

Edward and the 10th Queen's were billeted at Brandhoek as part of the 41st Division commanded by Major General Sydney Lawford, and on 28 September took part in a huge Allied push south-south-east from the line of the Ypres-to-Zonnebeke road. The advancing front covered some four and a half miles, and this would have been Edward's first experience of such a major attack. The 10th Queen's were behind the first line in support, clearing dugouts, taking charge of prisoners and securing arms depots in the wake of the attacking force. Torrential rain didn't hamper the attack, which came without a preliminary bombardment so had a crucial element of surprise. Having marched for most of the day to reach the assembly point at Hill 60 at 3 p.m., the 10th Queen's set off in support of the advance until they reached a line between Zandvoorde and Kortewilde, south-east of Ypres and about half-way to the River Lys. By the time they got there they had sixty-three German prisoners, sixteen captured machine guns, some field guns, a howitzer – and a bus. The whole attack had been a tremendous success. Fred Dixon remembered being on Hill 60.

'On the afternoon of 28 September 1918, after we'd taken over from the first wave of troops that had attacked Hill 60, I found myself on the crest of the hill with a Morse flag in my hand. Our companies were working their way down the east side of the hill when Lieutenant Stone came to me and said he wanted me to find B Company, because they couldn't find them. The first thing that occurred to me was to start flagging "B Coy", so that's what I did. Well, they soon opened up a machine gun on me and I was soon on the earth. I crept forward on my stomach down the slope of the hill, and one of the first things I came across was a disembowelled Jerry ripped up by a shell. About 100 yards beyond the dead German I became the target of a Hun machine gun, coming from the direction of what had been a big house called the White Chateau, which was only a heap of rubble at this stage. There was a ditch handy so I crawled along it. I thought they were shooting at my pack – they must have been able to see it above the ditch as I crawled along. But after a few yards I heard a terrific explosion, and there was one of our 18-pounder guns opening up at this Boche gun. It seemed an artillery officer and sergeant were having a duel with this machine gun, so they weren't actually firing at me at all. The Boche would fire a burst and then stop. When that happened, our officer and sergeant would come out, push a round into the breech and let off a shell at the machine gun, and so on. This went on for quite a bit, and there was I stuck in this ditch. Eventually, when things eased up a bit, I moved forward and found B Company. The Captain sent back a runner with me, the runner went first, and when we came within this target area we were held up by the 18-pounder firing over our heads. Then we came to a track where there was no ditch so we were briefly very exposed. I said to the runner, "In a minute, get up and go over to the other side of the road and you'll find a ditch there. Run over to it and get in, but leave room for me to follow you." He did, and there was a burst of machine-gun fire and a shell in return. Then I shouted to him, "I'm coming!", got up, ran across the track, threw myself full length into the ditch, with bayonet fixed, and unfortunately stuck the chap right in his bottom.

'He wasn't at all upset about it. He didn't blame me. There we lay in this ditch, with this duel over our heads, while I tidied him up with a field dressing. I got his trousers down and strapped him up, and then we crawled away. A few minutes afterwards, the 18-pounder sent a shell over and there was no reply, so I suppose the Boche gunners had had it.'

The following day, the battalion was detailed to assist an attack on a line along the Ypres to Comines Canal, slightly west of their position. The Germans put up more of a resistance than initially expected, after the galloping advance of the previous day, but again the Allies were successful, and on the morning of 30 September Edward and his cohorts reached the banks of the Lys between Comines and Wervik.

From there, they moved a couple of miles east to Kruiseke, coming under heavy shelling and rotten weather for the whole of the first week of October, before finally arriving at Douglas Camp, with four days to rest and prepare for the Battle of Courtrai.

Bradford's Horace Calvert wasn't far away, a few miles south-east at St Leger, as part of the huge effort to push the Germans back from the territory they'd gained in the spring: 'This was a daylight attack and we were constantly fired on by machine guns. I was carrying a Lewis gun with a fellow called Bamping, and as we were approaching the German line we could see them all lined up and firing. Bamping set the gun up and started firing at them, and he did enough that they cleared off. We got into these trenches and there were a lot of huts around as well. Six of us went into one of the huts with a sergeant, who said to me, "The machine gunners are busy over the flanks so watch that side there." I left the hut with the gun and kept well down. Almost immediately I could see these Germans not fifty yards away, having a look round. I knew what they were doing: they knew we were there somewhere and wanted me to open fire and give away our position. The other chaps were in the hut with the sergeant, out of view, and I was the only one left in the open, but there was a lance corporal with them and, not realising there were Germans so close, he stood up at the window of one of these huts to have a look out. I shouted at him to get down, but it was too late: they got him right between the eyes.

'Then I heard a noise behind me and it turned out there were two Germans inside another hut, fully armed, so close they could have shot me for what I knew. I called on the sergeant because I heard them scattering back inside. I couldn't leave my post, so the sergeant went in and brought them out and they were youngsters, only about eighteen. This had been their first attack and it had failed. It turned out they were bank clerks from Berlin – they'd been called up and only had about three months' training. They were right pleased to be prisoners, because they didn't like what they'd seen.

'We stayed there until it was dark. The Germans didn't know where we were, and when they were busy trying to reorganise themselves we managed to get away under cover of the dark. We collected some of our wounded and a few wounded Germans, took a few prisoners as well and by the time we got to our lines there were more of them than there were of us. They'd just given up.'

In September, Horace and his unit went towards the Hindenberg Line, ready to attack the Canal du Nord, a dry canal. A huge barrage was planned to precipitate the infantry push: 'On the way up I saw that the 18-pounders were wheel to wheel. The gunners said they were going to put a shell on every three yards of trench and keep it up as long as they could. At five past four in the morning the barrage started, and off we went. The Coldstream Guards were leading and we were behind them.'

Horace had to descend scaling ladders into the empty canal, effectively a concrete-lined trench some twenty feet deep, then place the ladders on the other side and climb up on to the bank. The pace of the advance, coupled with the extraordinary pounding of the barrage, had caused the Germans to retreat with haste, and when Horace emerged from the dry canal he could see in the distance the German artillery being pulled out and the soldiers retreating.

'I went across an open field and right in the centre was a gun,' he said. 'You couldn't see it until you got on top of it, and it hadn't been fired – we'd been too quick for them.'

On arriving at the now-vacated German trenches of the Hindenburg Line, Horace was impressed with what he saw: 'I've never seen a trench system like it in my life. Tremendous strength. Well built up, immaculate firing positions and dugouts, plenty of dugouts.'

They settled in to facing the Germans, but their retreat was too quick for the British even to properly establish themselves in a position: 'The Germans were so far away that they were firing machine guns, but the bullets were dropping short – they weren't even reaching us. We waited in this road for a while but didn't see a single German; they'd all gone. In the distance we could see the town of Cambrai, and it was on fire.'

For James Watson, the advance had a curious soundtrack: 'It was a Sunday night, I remember, and I could hear church bells in the distance. We went over the top between 6 and 7, as the church bells were ringing somewhere across the fields. Ahead of us was a dry stream, in which was a little boat, turned on its side with five Germans behind it: a corporal and four privates, who were giving us a great deal of trouble. We went forward to get them and had gone no more than a few yards when my mate was hit. His tin hat went up and he dropped down dead, never made a sound. I put the machine gun down on the ground: I had an idea where these Germans were and I gave a burst from this Lewis gun towards where they were hidden. All of a sudden these five Germans came up out of the boat with their hands up, going, "*Kamerad! Kamerad!*" I would have killed all five of the buggers but the sergeant told me, "No, we'll take them prisoner."'

The war was reaching its final stages, but Bill Holmes would be going home sooner than most. He was in the line near Zillebeke Lake, south-east of Ypres.

'The Ypres section was the worst part of the line,' said Bill. 'The Germans had shelled the lake, and it had flooded the ground all around. The engineers banged eight-foot piles into the mud in two lines, until there was six inches showing, and put duckboards over them. They zigzagged all over the place because straight lines would have helped the Germans find a range with their shellfire.

'I'd come over the mud and was in the trench when, suddenly, I felt as if I'd been hit by a blacksmith in my left side. I was in agony. The sergeant came by and said, "What's the matter with you, Bill?" I said, "I've been hit." He said, "You couldn't have been. There hasn't been a shot fired in the last hour." But, putting two and two together, I think a German sniper with a silencer had aimed at my head, missed and the bullet had hit the back of the trench and ricocheted into my left side. They had to get me out on a stretcher under machine-gun fire, and they dropped me and they all got flat on the ground. Eventually they got me to a French château, half a mile away.

'The surgeon couldn't find the bullet and I was in agony, so they gave me a cup of tea and gave me heroin. The nurse put the heroin into my thumb and I'd no sooner drunk this cup of tea than the whole scene changed: I could see flowers twenty foot high, lovely fountains, and I felt so well for a whole hour. That bullet was in my body for seven years, lying close to my spine. It was 1925 before I insisted they take it out.'

Early in the morning of 13 October, the 10th Queen's travelled by train to 'Clapham Junction', a point to the east of Ypres, and then began their advance in the evening under heavy shelling, sustaining a number of casualties. The next day dawned, shrouded in thick fog, with the Allied barrage being met by considerable German artillery in response. The poor visibility caused great disorientation among the Queen's and their fellow battalions, and the fog and smoke lifted to a scene of utter confusion – and an unfortunate proximity to enemy machine-gun positions. There were yet more casualties. Luckily, the battalions were able to reorganise, continue the advance eastwards and take out the German batteries. Once this had been achieved, the Queen's were taken out of the line for a few days' rest, ahead of the next big push, to secure the River Scheldt.

As my last morning in Ypres dawned and I prepared to set off for Courtrai, I knew my path was drawing ever closer to Edward's. I was catching up with the shadow I'd chased all the way from Kensal Town.

19

'IF EDWARD WAS EVERYMAN IN THE FIRST WORLD WAR, EQUALLY HE WAS EVERY ORDINARY MAN WHO'D FALLEN IN BATTLE OVER THE CENTURIES'

As I left the peaceful idyll of the Ramparts Cemetery imbued with an illusory joy at its location and vista, barely a hundred yards away I was brought back to the reality of the war with a jolt. The Ramparts War Museum won't be there much longer – the collection is being packed up and shipped to England – but it's an extraordinary place. For one thing, there aren't many museums of any kind accessed through a pub where you buy a token that admits you through a turnstile into what appears to be a large shed in the back yard.

Museums spend fortunes putting together the right kind of informative experience. They must engage as much as educate, entertain as well as elucidate. It's not about looking at objects in glass cases any more, it's about interaction and involving the visitor rather than preaching to them. The modern museum needs the visitor to leave feeling as if they've had an all-round experience, and not been walked around a giant glorified textbook. The Ramparts War Museum achieves this end result spectacularly, but it does so by breaking all the rules.

I hadn't expected a great deal, it must be said (the official tourist board literature points out that this is a 'private museum', a term that always seems to me to contain an implied 'so don't blame us'), but inside it I spent one of the most memorable half hours of my entire journey. Once through the turnstile you're plunged into gloom and immediately become aware that you're walking on trench-style duckboards. The corridor is narrow and you're beneath a low roof: it's claustrophobic, intimidating and oppressive, and playing through unseen speakers is the thump and boom of artillery shells on a permanent loop. You are, in effect, in a First World War trench rather than a converted shed in a pub beer garden.

Within a minute of heading down the twisting, turning passageway, I had completely lost my bearings: I didn't know which way I'd come, nor did I have any great confidence in which way I might be going. I was disorientated, yet at the same time utterly spellbound. This was a proper, old-fashioned museum: you're led through displays that feature mannequins in ill-fitting uniforms and unconvincing poses, yet you're utterly convinced, mainly because nearly all the materials are 100 per cent genuine, from motorcycles right down to belt clips and everything in between. The information is on typed cards so old the edges are furred, and it's so dingy in there that I had to use the light of my mobile phone to read them.

It's a museum that doesn't sanitise the war, either; there are some gruesome photographs of tangled corpses that loom out of the gloom without warning. It was a raw experience, lost in the passageways with the sound of the guns, being greeted by hard-hitting displays at every turn, all of it bar the mannequins themselves entirely authentic. There are no touch screens, no holographic heads of hammy actors telling stories; it's just you and the *stuff*, take it or leave it. And in the Ramparts War Museum you've no choice but to take it. Eventually I found a door marked 'exit' and stumbled out into the blinding sunshine of the courtyard again. The sound of the explosions stayed in my head for a long time afterwards: I'd been in the 'trenches' for no more than half an hour, but it had affected me far more deeply than I could ever have anticipated. It was on a pretty low-wattage level, and the comparison is admittedly trite, but as I walked back into the bright, airy bar where locals sat on stools and watched a cycling race on the television I felt I understood a little more of what it must have been like to walk into Talbot House or Ginger's after a turn in the line. I craved the normality of a beer (the bar sold a special 'Peace' beer) and a bit of televised sport, as the booming of the guns – just half an hour's worth of a recording in a museum, remember – still played out in my head.

Having gathered myself together and called in at the Grote Markt's newest establishment, Ypres Burger, for lunch (according to the menu on the tables, they offered both a Poppy Burger and a Double Poppy Burger, which sound, erm, dignified), I made my way to the centrepiece of Ypres' First World War commemoration, the newly refurbished In

Flanders Fields Museum. Located in the Cloth Hall itself, the museum promised to be the antithesis of the Ramparts Museum. Expensively redeveloped, this is the ultimate modern museum experience: multimedia displays, interaction and personalised technology. I confess that I rather feared the worst, that this might be a museum to have had any sense of depth or character workshopped, consulted and focus-grouped into oblivion – especially when I was handed a rubber wristband emblazoned with a poppy motif at the ticket desk that promised to be the key to my personalised interactive experience.

I spent a good two hours or more in the museum, its exhibits ranged beneath the vast vaulted roof of the Cloth Hall, which highlighted the contrast between the ultimate victory of Ypres and those catastrophic four years. You could look at the devastation and meticulously designed killing machines on display, then look up to the enormous space above your head and the beautiful vaulted ceiling that had risen from the rubble and closed over the war that had destroyed it – the finest possible symbol of regeneration and renaissance.

In Flanders Fields has a lot of history to cover, and it pulls it off very well, giving a comprehensive overview of the war in a form accessible to a non-expert like me without ever becoming dull or repetitive. British uniforms and weapons are shown alongside German, French and Belgian equivalents. The stories are told of the civilians who found the most devastating conflict in history rampaging across their land and through their homes, as well as those of the soldiers in the trenches.

The ever-present foreboding soundtrack, composed and recorded by the Nottingham band Tindersticks, stays just the right side of being intrusive, evoking an appropriate feeling of dread and tension that never overwhelms, but merely underpins.

Extra gravitas – if it were needed – is provided by the realisation that the artefacts on display, from machine guns and gas masks to what appear to be small lumps of rusty metal, were turned up here, in these Flanders fields. That the Cloth Hall now provides a roof over the same shells that reduced it to a pile of rubble is another neat illustration of how and why the museum is there today. A display of objects recovered but not used in the restoration of the town is a highlight: a giant 'X', the Roman number ten from a destroyed clock face, and small pieces of medieval detail from a building; items not designed to be seen and scrutinised from close up, but which are now relics representing the rebirth of Ypres.

For me, however, perhaps the most captivating thing in the whole museum wasn't a piece of equipment or a cutting-edge technology audio-visual display, it was a simple, silent video playing on a loop inside a display case. It's footage of the discovery of a flooded trench, north of Ypres at Boezinge, at the end of the last millennium by a group of amateur archaeologists called the Diggers.

The trench – now known as Yorkshire Trench – is restored and open to visitors, but the entirely silent video if its discovery has a remarkable immediacy. The film is from around 1998, and it's genuine living history. Although it's in colour, the knee-deep mud that covers everything lends a monochrome feel to the footage. The film shows men in oilskins inside a newly opened dugout reaching into the cement-grey water and pulling out object after object: a small shovel, a thigh-length wading boot, a tool bag with an oil can. There's a flash of bright blue: a glass bottle. A roll-out leather wallet containing a first-aid kit. There's a gas mask, rifle, grenades and rounds of ammunition. Every revelation from the murk is given extra poignancy by the silence and the realisation that these objects – some of which were on display around the screen in the case – had been last touched and held by their original owners nearly a century earlier. Somehow, the decades of distance increased the immediacy of the finds, as if the objects were being handed over by the men who'd owned them. I didn't make it to the Yorkshire Trench itself, but the photos show it restored and in the sunshine, looking perhaps too good; it was the dark, cold and cloying knee-deep mud of its discovery that made the First World War feel closest of all.

It was early on a Sunday morning when I walked through the Menin Gate, crossed the moat and turned south. There was a direct route east to Courtrai from Ypres, but I'd noticed on the map that if I headed south I'd pass through places mentioned in the 10th Queen's battalion diary. I'd follow the old Ypres–Comines canal to Comines and then make my way along the Lys to Courtrai: a much longer route than the direct one but, while lying on my bed in the Old Tom with the map spread out, I'd decided on a whim to amend my plans. I hadn't set out to follow Edward's route through Flanders – I'd just planned to walk to his grave – but the battalion diary showed that at the end of September, five weeks before he was killed, the 10th Queen's marched from Brandhoek to Hill 60, and then on to Comines (now Komen), Wervik and Courtrai. That, I'd decided, would be the route to take.

Heading away from Ypres, I turned south-east to Zillebeke and walked alongside the lake as behind me the church bells sent their deep, sonorous tones across the countryside. I paused briefly in Zillebeke Churchyard Cemetery, where a small clutch of Commonwealth War Graves Commission stones marked the final resting places of some British officers who'd died here in 1914. Most seemed to be cavalry men killed in the early weeks of the war, as the realisation dawned that the old days of sword-waving mounted charges were over in the new age of weapons technology finely tuned for nothing more tactical and chivalrous than mass extermination.

A little bit further on, around three miles from Ypres, I reached Hill 60. Formed from the piled earth left over from the construction of a nearby railway line during the 1850s, it was always more of a hump than a hill (it was apparently named Hill 60 because it's sixty metres above sea level), but in this part of Flanders anything above spirit-level flatness is regarded as a rival to the Matterhorn. Its height made Hill 60 an important part of the salient, and it was the scene of some of the fiercest fighting of the war. The hill changed hands several times: the Germans took it from the French in December 1914, but the British claimed it in April 1915 thanks to an assault that benefited from the hill being mined from underneath. The Germans launched gas attacks a month later that led to many casualties and their retaking of the top of the hill, but in 1917 more mine work, particularly that by Australian tunnellers, led to the Allies reclaiming Hill 60 at the start of the Battle of Messines. It changed hands again before being ultimately claimed by the Allies on 28 September 1918, following an attack in which Edward was a participant.

After the war, the hill was left pretty much as it was. Souvenir stalls sprang up in the 1920s, selling some of the enormous amount of detritus that littered the place, while a quirky, popular museum remained at the edge of the site for many years (a modern café stands there now). Today the whole site is administered by the Commonwealth War Graves Commission, because Hill 60 is essentially a mass grave for countless dead from both sides, most of them still buried deep inside the hill.

It's a peaceful place now, pleasant even, with the look and feel of a park. To the untutored eye the only difference between Hill 60 today and a suburban recreation area is the curious nature of the landscape: the hill undulates with craters that range from enormous ones left by the mines to slight indentations made by smaller artillery. Trees and bushes have grown up over the years as nature slowly reclaims the land, furring over the craggy crater-edges with grass and smoothing down the sharp corners of conflict. When Edward was here it would have been a hellish sea of mud, puddles, rusted barbed wire, lumps of metal, shell fragments, trenches and dugouts. I sat for a while with my legs hanging over the rim of a large crater while occasional snatches of commentary and laughter drifted through the trees, as a tour guide explained the history of gas masks to a coach load of English school children.

I continued south, picking up a path alongside the old Ypres–Comines canal. I knew from the battalion diary that Edward would have come this way as the 10th Queen's helped to secure the line of the River Lys at Comines. The canal, long redundant, was stagnant, flyblown and swampy: trees swooped low over the murky water in a way reminiscent of the Louisiana bayous rather than of a former key trading waterway.

I arrived at Comines and turned east to follow the Lys to Courtrai. The Lys also serves as the border with France, making Comines a divided town. The Belgian side, on which I walked, was quiet, but on the French side there was some kind of hootenanny going on: looking across the river, I could see between buildings yellow-jacketed stewards and metal barriers, and could hear the booming echo of a PA system. The noise followed me along the river for a good while, the thump of bass at one point giving way to a brass band playing 'It's a Long Way to Tipperary'.

I stopped to rest on a bench by the river in the afternoon, watching a long, covered barge move slowly in the direction from which I'd come. The skipper sat high in the wheelhouse and raised his hand in greeting as he passed. It was another warm day, and I'd threaded my waterproof jacket through a couple of loops on the outside of my rucksack, which lay next to me on the bench. I was only a day away from Harelbeke now, and I began to think about what waited for me there. I suddenly became aware that I'd brought nothing with me. I was so caught up in myself and my journey that I had brought nothing to leave with Edward, nothing to at least mark the fact that someone had been to visit him. Flowers seemed wrong somehow, and I wasn't sure if the CWGC would approve of anything even remotely ostentatious being deposited on the graves. As I thought about this I looked down and caught sight of something protruding through a tiny ventilation flap in the corner of one of my jacket pockets. It was the rounded end of a small pebble. I reached inside the pocket and, far at the end of one of its recesses, closed my fingers around it and pulled it out. It was small, flat, light blue-ish grey in colour and shaped like a half moon. I turned it over a couple of times and then remembered where it had come from. A few years earlier I'd written a book recreating great journeys from history on foot, including King Harold's 1066 march from the Battle of Stamford Bridge in Yorkshire to the Battle of Hastings. At the end of that journey I'd picked up this stone from next to the commemorative plaque in the ruins of Battle Abbey that marks the spot where Harold purportedly fell. It must have been in my pocket ever since, pushed right into the furthest corner and forgotten. All the miles I'd covered since, hundreds of them spent wearing or carrying that jacket, and the stone had been with me the whole while.

I thought back to that journey, starting at the battlefield where Harold had seen off the Viking threat for the very last time before receiving news that the Normans had arrived on the south coast. He'd marched his army south, far quicker than I'd managed, and I'd grown to admire Harold and his soldiers greatly on that journey. I'd seen a lot of England, too, passing through towns and villages that would have lost sons in that battle and often pausing at their war memorials to scan the list of names from the more recent conflicts. Finally, I'd arrived at the Hastings battlefield, where Harold and his army had come within a whisker of pulling off a second epoch-changing victory in the space of a fortnight, and stood on the spot claimed to be where he fell, feeling a tangible sadness at his demise.

It occurred to me that in Harold's army that day there must have been hundreds of lads like Edward in the *fyrd*, the equivalent of a territorial force: not full-time soldiers but primed to be called up at a time of need. On his journey south, Harold had sent word into the surrounding towns and villages, and they'd come, emerging from the countryside, ordinary men, poor men, joining a growing fighting force as it headed south to face a foe that threatened to transform and subvert their whole way of life – and not, as far as they were concerned, for the better.

For some, this was a political squabble among the elite involving territory, oaths and competing claims to thrones; for others, it was a necessary defence of a nation and a culture. A war just like any other, then, in which common-or-garden lads far better equipped for other things would die on the battlefield as either winners or losers.

I saw a neat symmetry in what I held in my hand: a stone from England, from a battlefield where ordinary men had died in great numbers. Where once I'd followed the journey of a king who was killed at the end of a losing battle, now I was following the journey of an ordinary boy killed at the end of a victorious war. There was a link between Harold and Edward running through a millennium of English history. This stone was perfect. It would be barely noticeable on the grave, and its provenance and resonance couldn't have been more appropriate. If Edward was everyman in the First World War, equally he was every ordinary man who'd fallen in battle over the centuries. I put the stone back in my pocket, heaved my pack onto my back and set off with a renewed feeling of purpose.

It might have been a long way to Tipperary when I left Komen, but it was also a long way to Courtrai, where I arrived eventually at the Hotel Damier on the town's Grote Markt, after a very long, arduous day's walking. There's been a hotel on this site since the fourteenth century, and a sign on the way in lists some of the hotel's more notable guests since, from the Duke and Duchess of Gloucester to Jimmy Somerville and Arthur Brown, who had '(The God of Hellfire)' helpfully appended to his name in case of confusion with any other itinerant Arthur Browns passing through. Whether The God of Hellfire was as pleased as me to see an enormous bath with a whirlpool facility in his room is very doubtful indeed. Certainly, the whoop I emitted when I saw it would not have been out of place on his biggest hit.

The restorative power of hot water and bubbles revived me enough to leave the hotel and take a stroll around the centre of Courtrai. It's another medieval town built on flax and textiles but, while it did receive considerable damage in the First World War, it was Courtrai's importance as a Nazi rail hub that saw an estimated 5,000 bombs dropped on it during the Second World War. The medieval belfry – all that remains of the old cloth hall – standing incongruously alone in the Grote Markt, chimed the hour as I left the hotel, but it was the only sound to be heard at the centre of the largest town in this part of Belgium. The square and the streets were all but deserted; I don't think I've ever seen a major town as quiet as Courtrai was that Sunday evening. I strolled through the empty streets down to the River Lys and stood on the bridge between the thumpingly impressive Broel Towers, a pair of conical-topped sentinels either side of the river that date back to the turn of the fifteenth century. I leaned next to the statue of John of Nepomuk, the patron saint of bridges, and looked east along the river. In the morning I'd walk alongside the Lys to Harelbeke and become Edward Connelly's first ever visitor. The water was still and the town remained quiet. It was only then that it truly dawned on me that I was nearly there. I'd been so wrapped up in routes and maps and walking and note-taking and sock-rinsing that it was only in the gloaming of a silent Courtrai evening, flanked by a pair of medieval towers that Edward would have seen during the 10th Queen's rest there two days before his death, that I could finally stop and think about what lay ahead of me. It was barely an hour's walk along the river to Harelbeke, no more than that. I was in the twilight of a day at the twilight of my journey in a place where Edward had spent the twilight of his short life. We'd come a very long way from Gadsden Mews.

20

'I FELT IT WAS A GREAT RESPONSIBILITY LEAVING EIGHTY WOMEN AND CHILDREN BEHIND TO DIE WITH NOBODY LOOKING AFTER THEM, BUT THERE IT WAS'

The battalion war diary of the 10th Queen's was kept meticulously by Colonel North, but as a lay person's reading matter it would never be in danger of troubling the bestsellers' list. A career military man of vast experience, North kept the battalion diary concise to the point of near-extinction: he could make a haiku look flabby and long-winded. Neatly typed, with place names in capital letters, the diary charts the movements of the battalion in brief sentences. One can imagine him in a dugout or billet, pipe clenched between his teeth, lifting the typewriter case onto a table, an upturned box or maybe even just his lap, depending on the circumstances, undoing the catch, lifting the lid, rolling a piece of paper into the drum and clattering away at the keys with his matter-of-fact account of recent events.

The diary gives the bare bones of Edward's final days until, at the end of the entry for 4 and 5 November 1918, which had described how the battalion had been relieved and were in billets, there is the bare addendum: '1 O.R. d. of wds.' One other rank died of wounds.

As obituaries go, it was pretty succinct. The names of officers killed were usually given, but the ordinary men were not afforded that luxury, understandably so, given the hundreds of casualties sustained in some actions: it would have been impossible to name everyone. They were recorded *somewhere*, that was all that mattered, and most would be given the immortality of a war grave headstone.

The diary is useful as a framework of events, showing that in October and November 1918, the war's final days, the 10th Queen's passed through Courtrai and travelled further east, driving the Germans back along a line between the River Lys to the north and the River Scheldt to the south. A detailed account of Edward's experiences during those last days can exist only in the imagination. The closest we can get are the battalion diary and the memories of the likes of Fred Dixon, who, as a linesman, was finding that the sudden change from trench attrition to galloping advances was keeping him very busy.

'Just before the armistice, on the left bank of the Scheldt, I was put in charge of the battalion telephone lines,' he said. 'When it was dark I didn't know the layout of the place at all, but we ran lines up to A and D Companies. They were in barns away from the river, but B and C were actually on the river bank. Me and this other chap ran out lines to A, D and C Companies, but we didn't know where B Company was. The Germans were shelling the roads so, being a country man, I set off across the fields, not realising there was a very wide irrigation ditch on the way. I took a running jump and landed right in the middle of it, up to my waist. I had another chap with me but he wouldn't jump, so I told him it was fine, he'd clear it. I knew he wouldn't and, of course, he landed right next to me. He climbed out and sat on the bank and cried like a baby. He was a big man, too, about thirty-five, had been in the Merchant Navy. I said, "Look, old man, you'd better shut up or I'm going to knock your bloody block off." Anyway, he stopped, and when we got back to the billet he took all his clothes off, dried himself and got into his blankets, although he shouldn't have done.

'The second in command asked if I'd got all the connections up and I said, "Yes, sir, all except B Company as I don't know where they are." By this time it was just getting light. So I went out again by myself – thinking the Germans would see two easier than they'd see one – taking a reel of wire and crawling along a ditch along the side of the road. When I ran out of wire I had to go back and get another reel, connect them up and go on crawling along this ditch. I came to a house and stood on the sheltered side of it. It was a lovely bright morning, good visibility, then I saw two figures standing outside a barn who were too far away to tell if they were wearing khaki or grey. So I stood up and sent as semaphore with my arms "RU", which any signaller would know meant "Who are you?" They replied "B Coy". So I started running as hard as I could across the field with the reel of wire on an iron bar, and bracing myself for a machine gun to start any second. I got as far as I could and jumped into a shell hole, landing on the body of one of our chaps.'

I can't help wondering whether this was Edward. Fred dates this to just before the armistice, and Edward was the only man from the 10th Queen's to die in the last couple of weeks of the war. 'One of our chaps' doesn't necessarily mean the Queen's, of course, but with so little of Edward to cling on to, and seeing this whole story filtered through his prism, it's inevitable that in my mind I would be putting him at the centre of stories like Fred's. It's still plausible that Fred Dixon, who we've followed from his Dorking childhood, spent a few brief, unexpected and unwelcome moments with the body of my grandfather's brother.

'I stopped and had a bit of a blow and wondered what to do, wondering if the Germans had seen me and trained a machine gun on the shell hole. So I took my tin hat off and put it on the end of my rifle and lifted it above the shell hole. Nothing happened, so I made a dash for it and got to these chaps from B Company with this wire. Instead of being pleased, they seemed a bit fed up with me and said, "You'd better bugger off quick before they start shelling." Well, I didn't need much encouragement.'

If there was a sense that the war was coming to an end, it wasn't necessarily expressed in the accounts of the fighting south-east of Courtrai. Clearly, the Germans were in retreat, and the men must have taken a while to get used to moving across open ground after being stuck in a trench for months on end, but there is no talk of the war reaching a conclusion. Fred Dixon's account continues imbued with the sense that death could arrive at any moment. Of course, for Edward it would, which creates a strange feeling when reading of Fred's experiences, knowing that Edward is in the vicinity of all of them and in the twilight of his short life.

Fred recalled: 'When we were advancing east of Courtrai towards the end of the war, one morning we were waiting in the cellar of a farmhouse near the village of Knokke, waiting for zero hour to arrive and commence the advance. The guns had opened up, Colonel North said, "Fall in, my army," and we trooped out of this cellar and across the fields in artillery formation, in line. Suddenly, from a ridge in front of us that had houses spread along it, came a burst of machine-gun bullets. There was a hedge to our right that we went through as if on a string, all as one man. It was remarkable. We were ready for it, not consciously, but all of us realising the danger and heading through this hedge and into a ditch.

'We'd been there for a while when I noticed Captain Toovey of D Company walking towards me. He had a lisp, and he said to me, "Dickthon, have you theen the colonel?" "Yes, sir, he's in the ditch up in front." He walked up, clear as day, to where the colonel was, came to attention and saluted. He was only twenty-two, Captain Toovey, and already had an MC and bar. He said to the colonel, "My company were in that barn and the Germans have just shelled it, so I've put them in that barn over there." The colonel said, "Yes, all right, Toovey." He [Toovey] saluted and returned to his company across the field. The thing was, they were machine gunning that field and dropping shells on it, and he calmly walked across it, not even breaking into a run.

'Another time, I was walking behind him and a sergeant when a dud shell dropped in front of us; it hit the ground but didn't go off. The sergeant dropped and so did I, but Toovey just stood there, looked down at us and said, "You thee, Dickthon? They can't kill me." I heard that he went to India after the war and died of sunstroke.

'While we were in the ditch I heard a cry, "Signaller!", from Colonel North. I crept over to him but didn't salute or stand to attention like Toovey had; I knelt beside him and he asked me if I had any wire. "No, sir," I said, "but I did see some German wire somewhere around here." "Get it in," he said, "because on that road over there is the advance brigade's telephone wire. I want you to tap into it and then bring me a telephone and line." I put on my hat and got over there hell for leather. I expected a burst of machine-gun fire at any moment but nothing came. I got this German wire and tapped into the brigade line, and the first thing the chap at the other end did was to tell me to get off the bloody line. I said, "Look, old man, I've been told to do this by the colonel of QUJ, hold on." I doubled back to the colonel; he got on to the operator and said, "This is Colonel QUJ. I want you to put me through to the brigade major please." "Yes, sir." Then I heard him say, "This is Colonel QUJ, will you put me on to the heavies? Are you the heavies? Here's a pinpoint for your attention." He told him where this machine gun was and almost immediately one 5.9 came over, and that was that. We got to the top and there we found the machine gun and two dead gunners. Both of them had fragments of skull stuck in their tin hats.'

In these final days of the war, Charles Ward was nearby at Westhoek Ridge. Like Fred, he'd noticed no let up in the fighting, even though the war was now mobile and the Germans were being pushed further and further back.

'There was no sense the war was nearly over,' he confirmed. 'And we saw plenty of action. A lot of fighting took place at Westhoek Ridge. We pitched tents and the Suffolks were nearer the ridge, and they got so many shells they had to leave the camp. We were the next camp and only got two shells, but both of them did damage. After a few days we got the orders to advance and everything was packed up and ready to move. We started advancing and reached a place called Houtem, where we stayed for one night. There, the boys did a lot of scrounging: one sergeant fitted himself up with ladies' silk underwear and got rid of his army stuff. In another place they found a chicken in a cupboard, somewhere else we found a box of Quaker oats and cooked it up for supper, unaware that it was loaded with something that gave us a tummy ache.

'We moved from Houtem to a place called Wervik on the River Lys, where there had been a German depot. In one dugout I looked in, the poor chap had been gassed – it was a horrible sight. The Germans had blown up the railway line every hundred yards, blown up all the bridges and left most of the villages badly damaged.'

'They cleared off back, we caught them up and there was a bit of action,' said William Dann. 'After a couple of days of chasing them down we came to a huge monastery with a moat round it. The Germans were holding that and they were rather in the way, so we had to flush them out. We went up close to it two nights running, practising going over the moat to get at it, and early on the third morning we went up to storm the place, well prepared and ready for the fight. Everything seemed quiet and, sure enough, when we got there the Germans had already gone. So that saved a lot of trouble.

'From there we just moved forward every day, coming across little spasms of action. We came across a farmhouse that had never been hit before and was well back in open country. The Germans were in there and they had a machine gun firing at us. Nearby was a little rise and a field planted with mangels. We crept through there on our stomachs, got to within twenty-five yards of the farm and found just in front of us a hole that had been dug, where men had clearly been before, that you could drop down into for shelter but would be briefly in full sight of the guns. We spoke to each other about it and said, Well, shall we chance it and slip over into that hole? Two decided to go over and one got hit because Jerry opened up as soon as he saw them. He was hit in the leg, badly enough, but he managed to get down into this place that had been dug out. Then everyone else followed except me, who was left with the Lewis gun. I thought, Oh, blow this, and I was that tired that I just toddled over. Immediately, there were bullets hitting the ground by my feet: it was sandy soil and I could see these puffs of earth as the bullets landed all round me. I got a bit of a spurt on and got down into this hole, where we found a man already dead. Eventually our artillery got the machine-gun post in the farmhouse and they were finished with. When we got there they were all dead, six of them, these Germans.'

Again, in William Dann's account there is little animosity towards the individual German soldier, which can possibly seem extraordinary to the layman, considering both sides were doing their level best to kill each other as quickly as possible.

'I'll give them their due, they fought well, the Germans,' he said. 'They were like us, I suppose, defending their own country just the same as we were, and they did their best, just the same as we did.'

As the 10th Queen's progressed across country, William Dann began to sense for the first time that the war had reached a different phase; that it might be coming to an end.

'It was November by this time,' he said. 'After that last little nest we got through we were still crossing open country, and we'd meet villages with civilian people who were good and helpful to us chaps. We also met some of our prisoners of war: the Germans must have left the door open when they retreated so they could leave if they liked. Some were in pretty poor condition, but some were reasonable, too. They were pleased to see us; we all shook hands and off they went.'

Lloyd Fox was an ambulance driver on the Western Front and was in the same area as the 10th Queen's as the war came to an end. But as the soldiers began to sense things winding down, for Lloyd there were still terrible things to come.

'The battlefield looked appalling,' he said, 'a sea of shell holes, tree stumps, shattered tanks and other bits of equipment, everything waterlogged and the road in a shocking state. I'd been warned that when I got to Courtrai the bridge would be under shell fire and probably unusable, and when I got there that's what I found. I had to go about a mile upstream to a pontoon bridge that took me into Courtrai, where I found members of my unit and a doctor installing themselves in a very large convent. There was no lighting or heating, but the rooms were huge and it was quite a respectable billet.

'On my second day at Courtrai I was sent out to find a wounded woman close to what was then the line held by the British, although everything was very fluid at that stage and nobody quite knew exactly where the lines were because the Germans were dropping back.

'I looked down into the Lys valley, where I saw this little village at the bottom, pulled up at a crossroads close to where the woman was supposed to be, and was promptly greeted by a German shell that landed in the ditch next to me and put one ear out of commission. I pulled away from the crossroads, found the woman, treated her and drove back to Courtrai. That afternoon, lorries started arriving at the convent, full of gassed women and children from the village in the valley I'd seen earlier. The Germans had laid down a lot of gas as they retreated, and it had gone into the valley. The civilians had retreated to their cellars for safety, but because it was an inert gas that was the worst place they could have gone, as it just sank into the cellars and followed them. Over a period of two or three hours that afternoon we had something like twenty lorry-loads of women and children arrive, about a thousand altogether, all of them gassed.

'We couldn't do much for them. There were no beds, most lay in blankets on the floor. We spent a good deal of our time dealing with those who had died, particularly the children, taking them down to the convent mortuary. Then, to make things a little worse for everybody, the Germans staged an air raid on the bridgehead at the bottom of the convent garden. Fortunately, the building wasn't hit, but those casualties who were well enough to notice what was going on were pretty miserable hearing the bombs coming down.

'The following day, I was taken by a young army doctor to a large hall in Courtrai, where we found over a hundred gassed women and children. It seemed all the men had been taken back by the Germans behind the line. There was just one old lady moving among them, trying to give them drinks, but they were terribly affected, their eyes were swollen, they couldn't see and their breathing was becoming more laboured as the phosgene set about their lungs.'

Faced with this horrific situation, Lloyd had to make an impossible choice: 'The object of our visit was to pick out twenty suitable cases who could be treated with a little more expert assistance and nursing at the convent. We reached the end of the building and the captain who was with me said, "It's up to you. Pick out twenty of the gassed people here that you think may have some chance of living and take them up to the convent with you." So there I was, just a youngster, being asked to pick twenty people whose lives might be saved, and all I could really do was pick twenty of the toughest-looking children. I took them to the convent, where a special gas unit had been brought from down the lines somewhere, but I don't think it was very effective. We washed their eyes out with bicarbonate of soda and the medical staff tried bleeding them, but I rather fancy that was a complete waste of time. They were all too badly gassed to be saved. I remember seeing one of the orderlies coming out of the ward in tears, saying, "I can't stand it in there any more; they're just choking to death." He was talking about the twenty I'd brought back: they were all black in the face and practically nothing could be done for them. I think in all there was something like 800 killed by the gas in that incident. It passed more or less unnoticed as this was the end of the war, and the news was more concerned with the Germans falling back.

'I felt it was a great responsibility leaving eighty women and children behind to die with nobody looking after them, but there it was.'

There it was. Lloyd Fox had been left with a terrible, heart-breaking and impossible choice to make, and it had all been in vain anyway. If Edward's death a week before the end of the war seemed pointless, then the deaths of a huge number of women and children are on a wholly different level of futility. These were people who had nothing to do with the war, whose village had been way behind the lines throughout the conflict and hence seen minimal action of any kind until the Germans retreated, lobbing gas shells in their wake. The villagers would have done what appeared to be the sensible thing when the shells began dropping and headed down to their cellars, not realising that the gas was following them, seeping through the floorboards and creeping down the steps, slowly filling the cellars and seeking out eyes, nostrils and mouths with deadly consequences.

Wilfred Heavens wasn't too far away in these final days of the war – a little further north, at Passchendaele Ridge, from where his battalion worked their way south-east. Like the others, he found himself chasing the retreating Germans and traversing the countryside behind the lines at a decent pace. At the end of October he wrote, 'During the afternoon we left the trench and reached the main road leading to the next village. As we approached we were met by a batch of civilians who greeted us joyfully, exclaiming, "*Allemands partis! Très bon!*" These were the first civilians we had encountered during the whole advance. The Germans had apparently given up the idea of taking the civilians with them, which showed they were in a deuce of a hurry. We passed through the village, bore to the left and entered a field on a high piece of ground. We could see the town of Courtrai lying below in the distance.'

The Germans might have been retreating but they certainly hadn't given up. There was still great danger from artillery and machine guns, and the Germans still held positions. One night Wilfred and his colleagues were in foxholes, aware that even the briefest flicker of light could give the German gunners a position to fix upon. Hence even the lighting of pipes or cigarettes had to be done carefully and out of sight.

'One man lit a match,' he recalled, 'and for a fraction of a second the flame showed above the funk holes. We shouted as loudly as we dared for him to "put that light out", but the damage had been done. Five minutes later a shell screamed over the hedge and dropped into a funk hole next to the one the light had come from, and three along from ours. It was followed by piercing screams and the two occupants were killed outright, while the two men in the next hole were badly wounded. The man who had struck the light escaped without a scratch.'

Once they'd managed to move on, Wilfred's unit had to take a village that had been held by the Germans: 'Arriving at the main road of the village, we entered a corner house for shelter and found it occupied by three or four Belgian women, who immediately made us coffee. Just outside their front door lay a dead German. The women pointed to him and made us understand he was a beast. In the evening we entered another house for a rest. In the first room we entered, we came upon a scene that was surprising and unusual. It was a bedroom and the furniture in it was just the same as it would have been in peacetime. Two oil lamps were burning on the chest of drawers and bedsteads like long wooden boxes were fixed to the walls. The women occupants of the house were sleeping in these beds, and in one of them was an old grey-haired lady of over seventy, whom it appeared seldom left her bed. Scattered about on the floor, stretched out and snoring, were our chaps who had just come off sentry duty.'

By the time the battalion reached German-occupied Vichte it was beginning to seem as if the beleaguered enemy was starting to lose its stomach for the fight: 'As soon as we were ready we launched an attack upon the village. The only real resistance was from the enemy's guns, which sent over shells in all directions. His infantry seemed to be on their last legs, for they were taken prisoner in large numbers. The German casualties were numerous compared to ours, and we were kept busy carrying down the wounded. For every one of ours, we carried down at least four Germans. They seemed to have resigned themselves to their fate, for you could hardly get a response from them through word or look.

'The civilians of the village began to emerge from their cellars to have a look round. As we passed through the village street we were met by civilians at their doors, waving to us and looking quite happy. Just outside the village we reached a farmhouse and were about to enter it when we noticed a small doorway in the wall of the house just above the ground. Looking in we found it was a cellar and inside was the farmer, his wife and daughter. We beckoned them to come out and they entered the house and gave us milk to drink. When we assured them that the shellfire had stopped now, they lit a fire, made coffee and prepared a meal. In the yard at the back the daughter filled a pail with mangel-wurzels, opened the door of a shed and fed four cows inside. The coffee was almost ready when suddenly a battery of our guns opened up from some distance behind. The women dropped what they were holding and made a run for the cellar. It was some time before we could convince then that it was our guns and there was no danger, and even then they would not leave the cellar.'

And then the war ended.

21

'DURING THAT LAST HALF HOUR BEFORE THE ARMISTICE, A CORPORAL WHO WAS WITH US GOT SHOT, IN THAT HALF HOUR, RIGHT AT THE END OF THE WAR, AND HE'D BEEN IN IT SINCE 1914'

On the night of 10 November 1918, Edward Connelly had been dead for nearly a week. I didn't know how, I didn't know where. I just had the Commonwealth War Graves Commission and the circumstantial evidence of the battalion war diary to go on, and had pretty much resigned myself to never knowing anything more specific than the date, a date that told me that the night before the Armistice came into effect he was in the ground. Hopefully the result of at least a half-decent makeshift burial rather than half submerged in a muddy shell hole or something. He nearly made it, but he didn't make it. Fortunately the other men here did make it, enabling us to hear their accounts of the last hours of the war.

On the same night, Wilfred Heavens was billeted in a village just outside Courtrai trying to get some sleep. Little did he know his night was about to be disturbed in the most unexpected manner.

'We had all just got between the blankets and were on the point of going to sleep, when faintly in the distance we thought we could hear a lot of cheering,' he said. 'Somebody remarked that the war was over, which was instantly quashed with the retort "Talk sense". Some time passed and we had almost forgotten about it, when we were roused, this time by cheering, close at hand. We lit candles, hastily dressed and went outside to find the cause. The regimental band had by now got dressed and were out in the village street playing for all they were worth. It was just 9 p.m. and the estaminets, which had only closed an hour ago, began lighting up and opening again. News had come through of the armistice.

'All along the horizon, where the front line was situated, Verey lights of all colours and descriptions were going up,' said Wilfred. 'Inside the estaminets, the men were dancing with the Belgian girls to the accompaniment of a penny-in-the-slot piano. After a few hours, getting tired of this, the estaminets closed and everybody everywhere retired once more.'

Lloyd Fox was still in the convent in Courtrai a few days after the trauma of the gassed civilians: 'I had a shocking cold and was sitting in the dark with a hurricane lantern in one of the rooms in the convent, and I thought it would do me good to put my feet in hot water. So I boiled some water and was sitting there warming my feet when news of the armistice came into the town. There was a lot of horn blowing. I forgot my cold and went down to the main square, helping to pull the German bandstand to pieces and make a bonfire to dance around. It was there that I had to deal with the last of my army cases during the war: an unfortunate soldier was hit in the face by a star shell fired by some drunken Americans who were roaming the streets firing their Verey pistols. One of them had hit this young man and killed him on the spot. That was my last casualty.'

Walter Cook was also dealing with casualties: 'We were in a village and I had five cases. People who'd been having a rough time, not wounded, they'd just had a rough time. The sergeant major dashed in and said there was an armistice. I've seen tired men move, but never as quick as these five – the shouting outside was terrific, and they wanted to see what's going on. A chap called McKillop, who was working with me, laughed and said, "Not much wrong with them, is there? Got any rum left?" I had three rations saved up. He said, "We'll have it all. I think I've got a drop left as well." We drank the rum, lay down and had a good sleep. That's how I ended the war: fast asleep, no worries.'

William Dann had reached the banks of the Rhine when news of the armistice arrived.

'I hadn't really expected the Germans to surrender; as far as we were concerned, we just had to carry on. We got to the Rhine and that was it, the war ended,' he said. 'At half past ten that morning we were standing at a point in the open country, when a despatch rider arrived and told our officer that the armistice was being signed and would come into force at 11 o'clock.'

If William had thought that this meant an end to random, poignant tragedy, however, then he was mistaken. The war may have been *over*, but it wasn't over: 'During that last half hour before the armistice, a corporal who was with us got shot, in that half hour, right at the end of the war, and he'd been in it since 1914. Goodness knows where that bullet came from, but it killed him. That was very sad. He was a nice chap, big man, very tall. He was in the Fusiliers, had come through the whole thing, stopped, heard the news of the armistice and then got killed.'

When the armistice was announced, Fred Baldwin was on his way home on leave.

'I came home on Armistice Day,' he said. 'I was on the first boat from Boulogne that day and we got the news half-way across the Channel. We got into Folkestone and every siren in the country was blowing away. We had Union Jacks on our trains up to Victoria and when we got there everyone was going mad. I had to get down to Bath, and two of us eventually got to Bath station with all our gear on. We went into a pub there and, before I knew it, I had six double whiskies lined up for me and so did my mate. When I got home my brother had just landed from serving in Ireland the same day.

'Although we'd got the news the armistice was going to be signed, no one could quite believe it. Even so, everyone was spewing and laughing and shouting – all the way home from the boat, everybody was mad. I remember more about that day than all the days on the Somme put together.'

As Fred Baldwin embarked at Boulogne, Fred Dixon was a few hundred yards away in hospital. His soaking in the drainage ditch and subsequent exposure to the elements in a wet uniform incubated an infection, and he was hospitalised with a temperature of 104 degrees Fahrenheit. Later, he learned how the 10th Queen's, now minus Edward Connelly, had heard the news.

'We were on the move forward in the line on 11 November,' he said. 'The battalion was marching forward along the road for fifty minutes at a time and then resting for ten every hour. They were on a ten-minute rest at the side of the road at about 11 o'clock when the brigade major came along and informed Colonel North that all hostilities would cease at 11 o'clock. We were at a place called Nederbrakel, and when 11 o'clock came our men went into the village as the Germans were leaving at the other end. They were acclaimed by the villagers – everyone went mad! However, the battalions were well disciplined and there was no risk of chaos. In the Irish general hospital the first time I heard that something must be up were the ships hooting their horns in Boulogne harbour. An orderly came in, took the shade off the lamp and said, "The war's over."'

The war might have been over, but if any of the troops thought they could throw down their arms, strip off their tunics and hightail it back across the Channel to the life they'd left behind, they were mistaken.

'The first to be demobbed were the special ones, like the military police who'd only just come out and were sent back immediately,' recalled Fred Dixon. 'Others of no importance, like myself, were kept out there. There was a bit of discontent; I believe there was some rioting in Folkestone and at base camps in France, but we were under orders to go on into Germany so we knew we weren't being released.'

Lloyd Fox wouldn't see Christmas at home either: he'd spend the cold winter of 1918 still in Belgium.

'I was another four months in Belgium, working mainly with civilians,' he said. 'It was very unpleasant; a very cold winter. We were billeted in an empty factory, very appropriately a woollen factory, with no heating. I had an orange, a rather prized possession, and the orange was as hard as a cricket ball. It wasn't easy to keep warm.'

Walter Cook had had to grow up fast during his time at the Front.

'I didn't have a youth, really,' he said. When he returned home to Finsbury Park he found work much harder to come by than before the war, even with the years of medical experience he'd gained at the Front.

'When I came back there was mass unemployment,' he said. 'It wasn't much of a life going backwards and forwards to sign on and get money for doing nothing. In the end, I answered an advertisement for a lunatic asylum in Liverpool, and they took me on so I moved there.'

In the immediate aftermath of the war, William Dann remained as part of the occupying army in Germany posted to Kaseren, outside Cologne. The welcome wasn't particularly warm: 'When we got there the German civilians gave us nasty looks. The officer came round with a troop of men to billet them with civilians in different houses. One woman was told she had to have two men and she swore at him, saying she wasn't having a single British soldier in her house. The officer said, "Oh, really? Well, you can have three, then."'

Still recovering from his gassing, Alan Short was at the hospital in Squires Gate outside Bolton when the armistice started.

'It was announced at 11 o'clock and everybody broke out of the hospital, went down to the centre of the town and had quite a time down there,' he said. 'It felt like being reprieved from a death sentence. I met my friend who was in the Royal Army Medical Corps and we enjoyed quite a day, visiting the pubs. Of course, the girls all made a fuss of us. I was at Squires Gate until December and then was sent down to Sheppey in Kent. I anticipated getting my demobilisation ticket there, being disabled by the gas, but they found out I could write and I was made an assistant company accountant to A Company. I'd hoped to get out of the army straight away, because anybody who'd been in hospital for a month at the time of the armistice was entitled to be demobilised, but it took me until April 1919 before I could go to the Crystal Palace demobilising centre. You had the option of getting a new suit or £2 in lieu. You also received £2 if you returned your greatcoat, and a lump sum commensurate with your length of service. Altogether I think I got £20. I had to go in front of the regimental medical officer, who examined me and reported that I had a "slight cardiac" with a 20 per cent disability. I got 12 shillings a week disability as a result.'

Alan called at his previous employers Union Castle to see if he could return to his old, pre-war job – which must have seemed like a lifetime away – but found no openings. Eventually he managed to find employment at a firm of chartered surveyors, where he began work on 26 May 1919 – his twentieth birthday.

Fred Dixon also struggled after his return, as he found that, for all the lip service paid to the brave boys at the

Front, when it came to finding work an army record could prove to be a disadvantage.

'I came back in April 1919 and managed to get a job with a firm of manufacturing stationers in Finsbury,' he said. 'That didn't last long, and I was out of a job for eight months, during which time I drew the dole for 15 shillings a week. In 1920 there were about a million people unemployed, and I applied for a job at the Ministry of Labour in Whitehall. I went before a board of old men for an interview and just didn't stand a chance. They said, "I'm sorry, Mr Dixon, but you've no experience." I saw red, and I got up on my hind legs and said, "Pardon me, sir, but I consider that I've had more experience than anyone in this room."

'I remember going for a teaching job at Malden Village Church School. I was asked about my war service on my application, but I didn't go into it because I didn't think it was relevant. When I was asked if there was anything I had to say, I drew their attention to this, saying I didn't want them to think I hadn't had any war service because I had. They said it didn't make any difference, but then one of the women on the committee said, "Oh, no, we want to forget about all of that, don't we?" I said, "Oh, yes, madam, yes we do. But I was there so I can't." The chairman sneered that whenever any criminals were up before the judge in London they always plead that they were ex-servicemen. I said, "Well, I'm not a criminal and I'm not doing any pleading. Good day." But that was the attitude. It wasn't a land fit for heroes because the old men were still in the saddle.

'I started my teacher training in July 1921, but even when I completed it I found nobody wanted you because they thought you knew nothing. The women hung on to the jobs they'd been doing during the war and it was the same with the younger men, the ones who'd been too young for the army, so the older men coming back just didn't have a chance.'

Fred eventually found a teaching job, rising to be headmaster of a local school until his retirement in the 1960s. In his later years he considered the nature of the things he'd done and the things he'd seen during his war service. In the calm and quiet of suburban Surrey, half a century after the event, the horrors of the trenches must have seemed like a different life, and he often looked back and wondered about the nature of his own psychology and that of his comrades.

'It's not an easy thing to talk about, really,' he said. 'I think if you look at the dictionary definition of courage it's just bravery or boldness, and cowardice is defined as faintheartedness, but it's not as simple as that. I do not regard fear to be a dishonourable emotion. I think fear is built into the very mechanics of self-preservation. Any man who says he didn't feel any fear in the front line is either a liar or an imbecile. Drawing on my own experience, I think a natural reaction to fear is action, which is manifested in either flight or aggression. The man in the trench can't run away and he can't indulge in a one-man offensive against the enemy of his own volition. I'm of the opinion that many cases of shell shock were caused by the infantryman having to sit down and just take everything that came his way without being able to do anything about it.

'Bravery in that kind of situation is shown when a man is fearful yet continues to carry out his obligations. That's bravery. Bravery should never be confused with rashness, however; that's something quite different, and both could get you killed. An officer once told us, "Remember, lads, you're no use to your side when you're dead," so I was never rash, but some people were. When we were at Scherpenberg at the end of the war, for example, several 5.9s dropped on the hill. A signalman from one of the companies wanted a nose cap as a souvenir so went out looking for one. Well, of course the Germans saw him, a shell came over and it killed him. He'd known how dangerous it was up there but still went out scouting for a nose cap, and of course that wasn't bravery, it was sheer foolhardiness. Now, there were intelligence men at battalion HQ whose job it was to go out looking for nose caps to send back for forensic work to try and get to the bottom of the technology. If one of those intelligence men had gone out at Scherpenberg, he would have been a brave man because under normal circumstances there was no way he'd have gone out looking for nose caps. But in that case his duty would have called him and he would have gone, and he would have been a brave man because he'd have been aware of the danger yet still done his job.

'I think fear becomes cowardice when one withdraws from one's moral obligations, but it can be accounted for. I wouldn't like to assess cowardice in anybody because it's something that can be affected by different factors: poor health, lack of sleep, physical wretchedness and one's mental and emotional equipment. I remember once I had bad toothache and asked the MO to send me to the casualty clearing station to have it out. It was at the time of an advance and he said no. When we were out at rest we were given sweet beer as an extra. None of the chaps liked it so I kept the bucket by my bed at night, and when my tooth plagued me I used to drink the stuff and hold it against the tooth. So, effectively I'd had no rest in that rest period, and when I went up the line I was as jittery as a chicken.

'On the other hand, I remember one night when I was told to find the signal officer of the 11th Queen's. There was no moon and it was total darkness, but I found the dugout and had to run a line across the face of a hill that I'd never seen before. It was night time, it was machine gunned and it was shelled. I ran out one reel of wire, then had to go back for some more, return, find the end of the wire, join them up and then run it back to our own office (the officer was so pleased with my success that he kept giving me similar jobs to do and said he'd put me in orders for stripes, but I didn't want the damn things). A friend of mine told me afterwards he was profoundly glad he'd not been chosen to go because he hadn't rated my chances of survival very high, but I hadn't felt that way about it at all because it was action. What I'd considered a routine job, my friend had considered an act of bravery, forming an opinion from inside a dugout where it was comparatively safe. It requires a good deal of moral courage to come from the safety of a dugout into a trench when the latter is being shelled, but once you're in a trench and you're over the top where there's no safety, things don't seem so dangerous because you've already achieved the ultimate in danger and there's not a thing you can do about it. There are areas of black and white in courage and cowardice, but there are very large areas of grey.'

Was Edward brave? Who can say. He could have been killed in an act of bravery but then just as easily he could have been killed in an act of rashness, or a momentary loss of concentration or distraction. That was the nature of the war, the kind of conflict that could see a man who'd come through the whole thing, all four years of it, learn of the armistice and still take a stray bullet that would kill him. Either way, Edward was just as dead as everyone else. If he'd seen out another week it could have been him sitting there in a suburban sitting room like Fred Dixon, the clock on the mantelpiece chiming the hours, recalling his experiences and his thoughts about the nature of the war and the things he'd seen and done. It could have been him enjoying a long retirement with his wife, with pictures of the grandchildren and china ornaments in a glass cabinet, sitting in his favourite armchair with the racing pages open by his side and casting his mind back to the extraordinary months of his war service.

Instead, through bravery, foolhardiness or just a random, deadly slice of rotten luck, the First World War killed Edward Connelly. The long life and happy retirement were taken from him in an indiscriminate instant in the mud of a strange country, mud in which he lies to this day. Whoever fired the gun or launched the shell in all likelihood made it through the next week and made it home. He may not even have realised he'd killed anyone, let alone Edward Connelly, the railway carriage cleaner from Kensal Town, that day. It's a strange feeling that there was a man out there somewhere who had killed my great-uncle, but as all the men we've followed through this story have confirmed, there was no malice against the individual soldier. It wasn't personal; he was just doing his job the same as they were and the same as Edward was. It's a strange dichotomy: taking somebody's life couldn't possibly be more personal, yet in the case of war it's an act that's entirely impersonal. As far as you're concerned, you're shooting at the uniform and what it represents, not the man inside it with a name, a family, a job, a past and a future. It's not a distinction I think I could make but, fortunately, I'll never have to. Edward died because of where he was and what he was doing; to the man behind the gun, the grenade or the bayonet he wasn't Edward Connelly, he was just the enemy. In different circumstances he could have turned out to be the best friend Edward ever had. No, the personal tragedy in Edward's death was the fact that he was subsequently forgotten, and lay unvisited and unacknowledged within a generation of his death. His own brother, my grandfather, had carried the grief with him his whole life, never mentioning it, never addressing it, never even telling his own son who carried Edward's name.

Unvisited, that is, until I arrived at his graveside, completing the journey from among the basketball court ghost of Gadsden Mews to a small British war cemetery in a little town not far from Courtrai. And I was on my way ...

22

'THE GHOSTS OF THE PEOPLE WHO NEVER WERE'

I was up and away early from the Hotel Damier. A market was setting up in the Grote Markt as I left, and Courtrai was coming tangibly to life after the somnolence of the previous evening. I crossed the river by the Broel Towers and turned east for Harelbeke. Ahead of me the sun rose slowly, throwing pale yellow beams down through a band of cloud, beams that shone straight down on my destination. The only sounds were my own breath, my footsteps on the path and birdsong. A cock crowed from behind a fence. A long, grey barge passed me in the opposite direction, sitting low in the water and making only the tiniest disturbance on the surface.

Normally, I like to set off at a good pace in the morning, get a few miles under my feet as soon as I can and ease off in the afternoon, but that day there was a hesitance to my steps. I was coming to the end of my journey; where the sunbeams landed lay Edward Connelly, nearly a century dead and in all that time unvisited, in a town whose name had meant nothing to me, whose name no one in the family had ever heard before until I found him in the records. Ahead was the town that was Edward Connelly's posthumous home and had been so for nearly a century.

I wasn't sure what to feel. Despite everything, all the reading and research, the late-night hours spent bathed in the blue-white glow of the computer screen with my neck stiff from poring over archive records, I knew nothing more of Edward Connelly than I'd found right back when he'd been uncovered in the family history. Yet here I was, about to visit his resting place. I felt like a child again, sitting in the back of the car, being driven to visit an elderly relative I'd never met, feeling nervous.

I crossed an iron road bridge, at the end of which was a sign informing me that I was entering Harelbeke. What was previously just a name on a screen was now a thriving town of shops, businesses and homes spread out between a river and a railway line. The sun had risen above the cloud, and I was sweating beneath it as I walked. I carried on through Harelbeke, past the town hall and past an enormous church, a lengthy roadworks trench beside me. A road turned off to the right – a green sign at the junction pointed to Harlebeke New British Cemetery. I was in a kind of daze now as I passed beneath a railway bridge, a train clattering overhead. And then, just beyond a hideous modern office building on the left, I spotted the now familiar rows of white stones set just back from the road, guarded by the imposing White Cross of Remembrance. I was just yards away now and these were the final steps of my journey. All the way from the former Gadsden Mews in North London I'd come, a walk that bracketed the entire life of the man I was here to see. I was barely aware of my own footsteps now and, almost before I knew it, I was through the gateway and feeling the tarmac give way to the softness of the grass. I'd already memorised the location of Edward's grave from the CWGC website so I knew roughly where I was going. He was just past halfway back, in the front row of a section of graves on the left-hand side. I found the row and began moving sideways along the stones, reading names that were all strangers to me, until I saw the familiar one, the one that matched mine and matched my father's. There, engraved on the stone, its familiar curves and lines leapt out at me, and seeing the family name on the stone in front of me triggered a bond. Standing in front of his grave, seeing his name there, I felt a connection to Edward Charles John Connelly. The letters swam slightly in front of me and I realised that I was blinking away the beginnings of tears. I hadn't expected the wash of emotion that emanated from somewhere in my stomach, rose up through my chest and caught in my throat. I pulled in a sharp breath that made my bottom lip rasp against my teeth and brusquely wiped the sleeve of my fleece across my eyes.

I stood and looked at the stone, the first person ever to come here and find Private E.C.J. Connelly of the 10th Battalion, the Queen's (Royal West Surrey) Regiment. It had taken almost a hundred years for anyone from his family to get here but, finally, after an inexcusably long time, we'd arrived. I reached into my pocket and pulled out the stone from the battlefield at Hastings, dropped to my haunches and laid it on the earth at the base of the stone, pressing it into the earth until it looked like it had always been there. Unsure of what to do next, I reached out and touched the side of the headstone, as if I was greeting an old friend with an affectionate pat on the upper arm.

'Hello, Uncle Edward,' I said. 'Sorry I'm late.'

This was it; this was the end. I'd never find out how Edward came to lie here – how and where he died. But at least I'd tried, and at least I'd completed a pilgrimage in his name that I hoped might at least partly atone for the near century of absent memory. Edward would remain a mystery; if no longer forgotten, then still an enigma. Did I feel I knew him any better from the accounts of his contemporaries? I certainly knew a lot more about the realities of life as an infantryman on the Western Front, which added a third dimension to the scratchy, speeded-up film of men in full battle dress stepping over barbed wire and walking into the mist, and photographs of dead-eyed troops staring at cameras from beneath tin helmets. But Edward himself? No. I was still projecting myself onto him, thinking about how I'd have reacted to situations and how I'd have felt in his position, but that told me nothing about the man himself. Seeing his name on the gravestone in front of me had caused an unexpected surge of emotion, but did I understand Edward Connelly, his war and his death, any better for being here? No, I had to admit that I didn't. There were still too many questions. But I was here. That was the main thing.

I stood up, took a step back and heard a voice from behind me.

'Good morning,' it said. 'What brings you here?'

Behind me stood a portly, grey-haired man wearing a sports jacket over a bright-red sweater, smiling politely. I was a little startled. This had been a solitary journey and a solitary moment; the last thing I'd been expecting was to be engaged in conversation in a cemetery. Especially when I had tears in my eyes. As it turned out, however, I may have reached the end of one journey but I was about to embark on another, even more enlightening one.

Fhilip Vannieuwenhuyze is that most invaluable of people: someone with a passion for history and a brain equipped to indulge it.

A high-ranking research chemist in his early sixties, Fhilip spends most of his spare time researching Harlebeke and its environs during both wars, and in particular the stories of the occupants of the Harlebeke New British Cemetery. He also visits the cemetery regularly, approaching visitors to see if he can shed any more light on their ancestors' stories or learn more himself. In addition Fhilip organises the annual Armistice Day memorial service at the cemetery. That morning, while driving through Harelbeke, he'd seen a sweaty, scruffy, whiskery man with a rucksack on his back heading into the cemetery, parked his car and followed me in.

After introducing himself, Fhilip saw whose stone I was in front of and said, 'Ah, Edward Connelly. Only recently I was researching him. I have a day off today – if you like I could show you some of the places he would have seen? I think it would be interesting for you.'

We walked back to his car. He searched several pockets for his keys, opened the boot, rummaged through some bulging files and pulled one out. We sat in the car and Fhilip told me extraordinary things. On 20 October 1918, he told me, Edward and his battalion would have reached Gullegem, a village north-west of Courtrai, after following a similar route to my own along the Lys from Comines, then marched south-east, looking to push the Germans further back from Courtrai. On 21 October they moved further forward to Bellegem and went into the line. For the next five days, the 10th Queen's were involved in fierce fighting, driving the increasingly demoralised Germans back at such a rate that the fighting would have been in the open. No need for trenches any more, just good field-gun positions for creeping barrages and covering fire as the infantry advanced relentlessly.

We buckled our seatbelts and drove off, stopping at a bridge over the canal that ran south from Courtrai towards Bossuit. A lane ran uphill alongside the canal and we began to walk up it.

'The 10th Queen's would have passed in front of us here on 22 October,' he told me. 'Where the canal runs in the open, in 1918 it actually passed through a tunnel under a hill called the Souterrain. The hill has since been removed, when they widened the canal, but in 1918 it would have been the easiest place to cross the canal, so it's certain that the 10th Queen's crossed at this point. Of course, when I say "easiest", that's a relative term: Edward and his colleagues would have been under heavy fire from German machine guns the whole time, and remember, there would have been little cover for them – no trees, like there are today, just a few buildings like that farm up there, where I have something to show you.'

We walked up the lane and I felt slightly dazed. Barely an hour earlier I thought I'd reached the end of my journey and of Edward's story. Now here I was being shown exactly where he spent part of his last days. To the left was the canal, to the right open fields and an old railway line. It was a strange feeling to know that Edward had passed in front of where I was walking, within yards of me at most; Fred Dixon, too, a man I felt I'd come to know well on my journey into Edward's life and war. We reached the farm building, and Fhilip brought me round to the gable end and pointed.

'Look there,' he said.

There were around half a dozen cavities in the brickwork, all about three inches across and a couple of inches deep, and randomly spaced across the right-hand side of the upper gable-end wall.

'Those holes were made by a German machine gun on that day,' said Fhilip. 'The gun that fired those bullets would have been firing at your great-uncle from somewhere on top of the Souterrain as they advanced.'

We returned to the car and drove further south-east towards the River Scheldt. The 10th Queen's had orders to make for and secure the river, which ran west–east, and keep forcing the enemy back.

After five days of this relentless mobile fighting – 'How and where did they sleep?' wondered Fhilip. 'How and what did they eat?' – Edward's battalion had reached the village of Avelgem, where they were finally relieved and withdrawn to Courtrai for three days' rest, until 2 November. The war was about to enter its final week, and so was my great-uncle. I wondered how he'd spent those final three days of rest in the town I'd left that morning, whether he'd walked in the main square as I had done and gone to look at the Broel Towers and the river. Did he know the war was almost over? Did he dwell on the heavy fighting of the previous five days, and had he lost friends and seen them die alongside him as they crossed the field where I'd just walked? Maybe he'd sheltered behind the bullet-scarred building I'd just visited as the bullets hit the wall, using it as cover to pause and regroup, and that's why the German guns had spattered its gable end with bullets.

On 2 November, Philip told me as we drove through the Flanders countryside, the 10th Queen's were sent back to the line near Waarmaarde. Here, he parked the car by a small marina and we climbed out.

'Now,' said Philip, 'now we are entering Edward's last hours.'

He spoke softly, like a medical consultant delivering bad news. I swallowed and looked around. We were at the bottom of a lane close to a tributary of the Scheldt, where a road sign on the wall of an old farm building said 'Ten Hove'.

'Ten Hove is where the battalion prepared for the next part of the attack,' said Philip. 'The Germans were on the other side of the Scheldt, and the 10th Queen's had to make their way from here, along the river bank, and try to push them back. Where we are standing is where that next attack would have started. Edward would have made his preparations here, and on 4 November the attack would have begun.'

He walked me along the bank of the tributary and then up a slip road that led to a dual carriageway close to a bridge that crossed the Scheldt. We crossed the road by a sign announcing the village of Kerkove and stopped by the edge of a slip road with a high vantage point over some fields. To the right was the Scheldt, a vibrant blue in the sunshine, and ahead were lush fields of various shades of green leading off about half a mile or so to a clump of trees and a small group of whitewashed buildings. It was an idyllic scene, even allowing for the traffic crossing the bridge directly behind us.

'So,' said Philip, indicating the vista in front of us, 'Edward would have had to cross these fields. It would have looked very different to this. It was November, it was cold, wet and foggy, and the fields would have been thick with mud, not green and verdant like they are today. The Germans had some very good artillery emplacements on the other side of the river, so it would have made crossing this field very difficult.

'I am fairly certain,' continued Philip quietly, 'that this stretch of land, between where we are standing and those buildings you can see ahead of us, is where Edward was killed. Probably by an artillery shell.'

I looked out across the fields, feeling ever so slightly numb.

'In the battalion diary it says he died of wounds,' continued Philip, 'so I think he must have been terribly wounded, possibly too badly to be moved, and died a little later, before he could receive specialist medical treatment.'

An empty feeling began in my stomach and started to spread.

'I'm also sure,' he said, 'that Edward would have been buried here. Not by his comrades in the battalion – they would have had to keep going – but by members of the second line, who followed once the Germans had withdrawn. They would have dug him a grave somewhere out there, buried him and made a wooden cross with his name, number and unit, and that's where he would have remained until, I think, 1922.'

Earlier in the day, Fhilip had explained how, when the Imperial War Graves Commission arrived in Flanders in 1921 to organise the Allied dead into dedicated military cemeteries, the Harlebeke New British Cemetery had been identified as the place to bury men who lay in the vicinity between the Lys and Scheldt. Some time in 1921 or 1922, a party would have arrived here to exhume Edward's body, place his remains in the small wooden box that would serve as a coffin and take him to Harelbeke, where he would be reburied – and where he lies today.

I'd thought the grave would be the end of my journey. Instead, it had been the start of a new and shorter, but far more intense one. The story should have ended in the neatly tended peace of a military cemetery, but instead it was ending here, next to a busy road looking out over farmers' fields, at the exact spot where Edward Connelly's short life, a life that began in the crowded slums of North-West London, was brought to a close. Not only that, out there somewhere in front of us had been his original grave. This is where he would have been lying when his parents, my great-grandparents, received the news that he wouldn't be coming home. They might even have received the news after the armistice, when they'd thought he was safe. He'd have lain here as the guns fell silent for the final time. He'd have lain here as the farmer and his family gave thanks for the end of the conflict in the farmhouse yards from his grave. He'd have lain here as across Europe people celebrated the end of the war. For a good three years the farmer would have worked the fields around him, maybe even greeting him as he passed by with plough or shovel.

He almost made it. If he'd managed to cross that field, the chances are that Edward would have survived the war. Nobody else in the battalion died that day, nobody else died in the next week before news of the armistice was confirmed. Indeed, he was the only member of his regiment to be killed in the last two weeks of fighting, making him the last of the 10th Queen's Royal West Surreys to die in the First World War.

He was unlucky, just so unlucky. A half mile of Flanders field between life and death, the only soldier killed during that advance, felled by a lucky shot or a brilliant one – it doesn't matter.

I stood staring out at the field for a while, saying nothing, not knowing what to feel.

'I think it's time for a beer,' said Philip.

The rest of the day is a jumble of images. When we got back to Harelbeke there was a terrific thunderstorm. We had dinner somewhere. He showed me Harelbeke's beautiful church with its amazing carved wooden pulpit until the priest came over and told us off for making too much noise during Mass. Then he drove me through what seemed like endless identical country lanes to where I was staying, the house of a lovely retired couple who took in occasional bed-and-breakfast guests. After a while, Philip and the kindly white-haired gentleman whose house it was realised they'd worked together in the 1980s. His wife brought us all a beer and Philip told the story of Edward again.

It had been a long, exhausting day and finally I retired to bed, where I know I had restless, feverish dreams about the First World War but can't remember any of them.

The next day, I bulleted back to London on the Eurostar from Lille, travelling as far in an hour and a half as I had in the best part of two weeks of walking. When we shot out of the tunnel near Folkestone and plunged into the Kentish countryside, I began to see spaces. Not physical spaces, but empty, imagined spaces, the spaces where people should have been: Edward's children, grandchildren and great-grandchildren, and those of all the other young men like him who never came home – the ghosts of the people who never were.

Edward Connelly wasn't a hero. It's a word that's horrendously overused these days, to the point of devaluing the real heroes. Edward Connelly was just a boy, barely a man, who came from an ordinary family and led an ordinary life until the day he walked into a recruitment office and took the king's shilling. What happened to him after that was extraordinary, an experience he shared with hundreds of thousands of others. There are Edwards in your family and there were Edwards in your town and on your street. There were Edwards everywhere you can think of, and many of them now lie beneath white headstones in Belgium and France. Many of their stories are untold and many will remain that way. Thankfully, we have the recorded memories of some of those who came home preserved by the Imperial War Museum, for it's in these first-hand accounts that the most immediate stories of the war are found. They're not 100 per cent reliable: they are recalled at a distance.

Dates and locations may have become mixed up, tales may have grown taller in the intervening decades, but it's through them that I feel I understand much more about what happened to my great-uncle: the things he would have seen, the sounds and the smells. Combining these with seeing the places in which these events happened, most notably the places where Edward spent his last days and hours, and ultimately died.

Edward's story is incomplete and ill defined, and is likely to remain that way for ever. But his war is that of every private infantryman, his experiences those of every young man who performed his duty the best he could, the brave, the terrified, the determined, the gung-ho, the sanguine, the resigned.

Edward Connelly is all of them, and all of them are Edward Connelly. For him the silence of a century is over. For thousands of others their stories are yet to be told. But they are out there. There is no need for any more forgotten soldiers.

BIBLIOGRAPHY

When I set out in search of my great-uncle Edward I knew little of either genealogy or the First World War. I found ancestry.co.uk invaluable regarding the former and the following books particularly helpful in alleviating my ignorance regarding the latter:

Bet-El, Ilana R., *Conscripts: Forgotten Men of the Great War* (The History Press, 2009)

Bridger, Geoff, *The Great War Handbook* by (Pen & Sword, 2013)

Holmes, Richard, *Tommy: The British Soldier on the Western Front* (HarperPerennial, 2005)

Holmes, Richard, *The Western Front* (BBC Books, 2008)

McCue, Paul, *Wandsworth & Battersea Battalions in the Great War* by (Pen & Sword, 2010)

Wylly, Colonel H. C., *History of the Queen's Royal (West Surrey) Regiment in the Great War* (N&M Press, 2003)

To locate your British and Commonwealth ancestors killed in the line of duty, visit the Commonwealth War Graves Commission website at www.cwgc.org.

AUTHOR'S NOTE

Visiting key places in both my great-uncle's and the Great War's narrative was an extraordinary experience, and months later I'm still trying to process the intense range of emotions it provoked. I can't recommend a visit to Flanders enough, especially if you have the slightest interest in or connection to the First World War.

Walking there might be a bit extreme, but if it demonstrates anything it's that Flanders isn't as far away as you might think: within a couple of hours of leaving London on the Eurostar you can be in the heart of the Western Front and, once you're there, most of the key sites are within easy reach of each other. The Visit Flanders website is the best place to start your planning: www.visitflanders.co.uk.

The Imperial War Museum archive in London is a remarkable treasure trove and I remain deeply indebted to them for permitting me to reproduce material from their archive. They have placed much of it online and made it freely available – lose yourself for hours at www.iwm.org.uk/collections-research. I am very grateful to their staff for their assistance, especially during the recent renovations when the place was practically a building site.

Finally, I am very grateful to the following people for their help and encouragement in the preparation and execution of this book: Natalie Jerome, Lizzy Kremer, Harriet Moore, Anita Rampall, Michaela Stedman, Bernard Sumner, Rich Payne, Emily Barrett and Mark Bolland. I am particularly indebted to the peerless and generous Philip Vannieuwenhuyze for his breathtaking knowledge and research in Harelbeke. Special thanks as ever to Jude, fellow-traveller and continuing inspiration.

Charlie Connelly, August 2014